Unlocking the Scriptures for You

TIMOTHY—PHILEMON

Knofel Staton

**STANDARD
BIBLE STUDIES**

 STANDARD PUBLISHING
Cincinnati, Ohio   11-40112

Unless otherwise noted, all Scripture quotations are from the *Holy Bible: New International Version,* ©1973, 1978, 1984 by the International Bible Society. Used by permission of Zondervan Bible Publishers and the International Bible Society.

Sharing the thoughts of his own heart, the author may express views not entirely consistent with those of the publisher.

Library of Congress Cataloging-in-Publication Data:

Staton, Knofel.
  Timothy—Philemon.

  (Standard Bible studies)
  1. Bible. N.T. Pastoral Epistles—Commentaries. 2. Bible. N.T. Philemon—Commentaries. I. Title. II. Series.
BS2735.3.S75   1988   227'.8   88-2139
ISBN 0-87403-172-9

CONTENTS

Part One

Proper Conduct
in the Household of God

1 Timothy

INTRODUCTION
TO FIRST TIMOTHY
AND THE PASTORAL EPISTLES

The letters to Timothy, Titus, and Philemon are the only letters in the New Testament that Paul wrote to individuals. Each of these four letters was written to an individual with whom he had been extremely close.

With the exception of Philemon, these letters have been referred to as the "Pastoral Epistles" since 1703, when D. N. Berdot coined the phrase. The term was not widely used, however, until it was popularized later by Paul Anton in 1726. Today the term *Pastoral Epistles* is a common title for these three letters.

The term *pastoral* goes back to the days of pastoring or shepherding sheep. Paul was functioning as a "shepherd" both to the evangelists, Timothy and Titus, and to the churches they served. Paul encouraged Timothy and Titus as well as discussing some specifics of both the qualifications and the treatment of the human pastors (shepherds, elders) of those congregations.

Some of the specific responsibilities that Paul outlined for Timothy in his first letter are as follows:

1. Guard sound teaching (1 Timothy 1:3).
2. Stress prayer (1 Timothy 2:1).
3. Outline the conduct of women (1 Timothy 2:9-15).
4. Spotlight the qualifications of the elders and deacons (1 Timothy 3:1-13).
5. Keep the essentials of Jesus spotlighted (1 Timothy 3:16).
6. Point out false teachings (1 Timothy 4:1-16).
7. Minister across age categories (1 Timothy 5:1-16).
8. Be sensitive to the treatment of widows (1 Timothy 5:3-16).
9. Be sensitive to the proper treatment of elders (1 Timothy 5:17-22).
10. Give proper instructions to those who are rich (1 Timothy 6:9, 10, 17-19).

The primary purpose for Paul's writing to Timothy was to remind Timothy of his relational responsibilities with and for God's people: "If I am delayed, you will know how people ought to conduct themselves in God's household, which is the church of the living God, the pillar and foundation of the truth" (1 Timothy 3:15). Paul was not talking here about conduct inside a church *building,* but relational activities and attitudes with the church *people.* A building is certainly not "the pillar and foundation of the truth." But people in whom Christ lives are!

Proper relationships that were necessary for Timothy involved the use of his gifts (1 Timothy 4:14) and a commitment to sound teaching and to sound conduct (1 Timothy 1:3; 6:11-14).

Pauline Authorship

It is rather common for several New Testament scholars to challenge the Pauline authorship of the pastorals. Some think that Paul could not have written the pastorals because they were written much later—even in the second century. Some of their reasons are cited below:

1. Some of the activities of Paul mentioned in the pastorals do not fit his travels in Acts. For instance, when did Paul leave Timothy in Ephesus and when did Paul ever visit Crete?
2. Some say that the letters combat a false teaching that was not present until a later period than the first century.
3. Some suggest that having a church organization with elders and deacons is a later development in Christianity than the latter half of the first century.
4. Some suggest that the literary style of the pastorals is not identical to Paul's literary style in other letters. For instance, of the 902 words in the pastorals, 306 do not appear in any of Paul's other writings, and 175 of them do not appear anywhere else in the New Testament. Consequently, some feel that this is evidence that the wording is not from Paul's style.

The first challenges to Pauline authorship came from some people as far back as the second century, Tatia and Marcion. However, these men were gnostic heretics who did not agree with much that Paul was writing, which contradicted their beliefs. So it was convenient for them to discredit Pauline authorship and thus discredit the pastorals as God's inspired Word for the church.

To question Pauline authorship with the above four criticisms is inappropriate. Those can be easily answered, as seen below.

Acts and Paul's Travels

Some of the historical data in the pastorals do not need to fit within the framework of the book of Acts. Luke's purpose for writing Acts was not to give us a blow-by-blow account of Paul's life. Acts is not a biography of the apostle Paul. The purpose of Luke in Acts is to show how Christianity became unshackled from Judaism to cross every kind of people-barrier and thus become God's means of salvation for *all* kinds of peoples.

Luke finished writing the book of Acts before Paul finished his career; so it is natural that many of the details he revealed about his later life are not in Acts. At the close of Acts, Paul had been imprisoned "for two full years" (Acts 28:30). But Acts says nothing of Paul's death. In fact, Paul himself was expecting to be released from that Roman imprisonment (Philippians 1:19, 25, 26; Philemon 22). Paul evidently was released around A.D. 62 and began to travel again. He may have gone to Spain. He certainly wanted to go there (Romans 15:24-28). Several ancient writers tell us that he did indeed visit Spain. (See *I Clement, Acts of Peter, Muratorian Canon.*) Evidently, after visiting Spain, Paul began to travel through Macedonia, Ephesus, and other parts. It was during this period that he left Titus in Crete (Titus 1:5) and Timothy in Ephesus (1 Timothy 1:3, 4). While in prison, he had planned to visit Philemon (Philemon 22) and probably did. He traveled into Macedonia (1 Timothy 1:3) and planned to winter in Nicopolis (Titus 3:12), and probably did. He probably came back through Ephesus to visit Timothy as he had promised (1 Timothy 3:14, 15). Later, he went to Troas, where he left his cloak (an outer garment for cold weather) and his scrolls (2 Timothy 4:13).

Paul said he left those personal items with Carpus, which probably means he had stayed with Carpus in Troas. It is possible that he then left those personal items, which seem to have meant much to him, because he was arrested in Troas. From that point he was transported back to Rome for his last imprisonment.

Paul said he left Erastus in Corinth and Trophimus—because he was sick—at Miletus (2 Timothy 4:20). These men may have been with Paul when he was arrested in Troas and accompanied him at the beginning of his last trip to Rome, or they may have been travel companions earlier and stayed in these cities before Paul reached Troas.

Paul probably wrote 1 Timothy and Titus between the two Roman imprisonments and 2 Timothy while in the second Roman

11

imprisonment shortly before his death. Consequently, we see a bit of Paul's activities after the ending of the book of Acts.

The False Teaching at Issue

Some who suggest that Paul was combating a false teaching that belongs to a later period suggest that because they feel the problem was to Gnosticism. But Paul's teaching relates to Judaism as well as to Gnosticism. Paul wrote about people's paying attention to myths and endless genealogies. Those were in Judaism. Paul early wrote about "teachers of the law"—that is certainly a reference to Judaism. Judaism and its teachings were the major threat to the spread of Christianity in the first century—not Gnosticism.

Church Organization

To suggest that it was too early in the life of Christianity to have elders and deacons is to overlook the fact that we find elders rather early in the book of Acts. Elders were in the Jerusalem church as early as Acts 11:30. Elders were appointed much earlier than the writing of 1 Timothy (Acts 14:23).

When Paul was traveling toward Jerusalem in Acts 20, he met with the elders of the church at Ephesus (Acts 20:17-38). So the church at Ephesus had elders early in its history.

Paul's Style

It is inappropriate to lock a person into the same usage of words in all of his writings. Although there are many words in the pastorals that are not in Paul's other writings, there are fifty words in the pastorals that are only in Paul's other writings and do not appear anywhere else in the New Testament. As a person continues to live longer, as a person continues to travel in other parts of the world, as a person is in various environments, he picks up words he has not used before. In addition to that, a person changes wording as he writes to different audiences. Here, Paul is writing to individuals, not to churches. A person changes wording as he writes to different situations.

The author of the pastorals was indeed the apostle Paul. He wrote 1 Timothy from Macedonia somewhere between A.D. 62 and A.D. 64.

CHAPTER ONE

A Letter From Whom?

1 Timothy 1:1, 2

The Writer

In the first century, a person did not have to look at the end of a letter to see who wrote it. The usual style for a person who wrote a letter was to put his name at the beginning of the letter instead of at the end as we do today.

If we followed that custom today, it might help us to know whether we want to read the letter or not. Probably, most of us look at the end of a letter before we even start to read it in order to see who wrote that letter to us. We can tell immediately who wrote this letter; the first word reveals the writer.

His Name

Paul is the writer. Actually, Paul had two names, "Then Saul, who was also called Paul . . ." (Acts 13:9). *Saul* was a Hebrew name; *Paul* was a Greek name.

Why two names? Some suggest that Saul's name was changed to Paul on the road to Damascus. But there is no evidence for that. In fact, we do not see anyone calling Saul by the name "Paul" until at least ten years after his conversion. Three days after Paul's Damascus-road experience, Ananias called him by the name Saul (Acts 9:17). He was still called "Saul" many days later (Acts 9:22). A decade later, he was still called "Saul" (Acts 11:25, 30; 12:25). The people at the Antioch church still called him "Saul" (Acts 13:1). The Holy Spirit referred to him as "Saul" (Acts 13:2).

The word *Paul* literally means little. Many have tried to conjecture why he was named "little." Some suggest he gave this name to himself to denote his humility. Paul did talk about the fact that he was the chief of all sinners and not superior to any others (Ephesians 3:8; 1 Corinthians 15:9; 2 Corinthians 12:11;

1 Timothy 1:15). However, the better likelihood is that Paul had both names from birth given to him by his mother. Perhaps Paul was a smaller baby than others, and thus his mother named him Paul as well as Saul. Perhaps a relative had that name, also. Or there may have been no significance to it at all. All of our names have literal meanings behind them, but many do not know what their names literally mean. So any coincidence between its meaning and the reason Paul was thus named may be totally superficial.

Most Hellenized Jews born in that period of time were given two names at birth. One was Hebrew; the other, Greek. Paul was born in a Hellenized area, Tarsus, but was brought up in Jerusalem (Acts 22:3). Saul did not begin to use his Greek name in a consistent way until he began his missionary journey penetrating Gentile territory. To use his Greek name in Gentile territory would give him enhanced rapport with the Greeks, but would not have disappointed the Jews who commonly used their Greek names in Greek territory.

We see a similar thing happening in the United States with various immigrants. Often a person with an ethnic name (such as a Japanese name, for example) will also begin to use an English name when living in the United States.

His Position

The word *apostle* in the first century was a common word used to denote the following:

1. Someone or something sent on a mission by someone else with higher authority.
2. While on that mission, the person sent was under the authority of the sender.
3. While on that mission, the person sent represented the person who sent him. In no way was he to represent himself.
4. While on that mission, the person sent was to do and to say what the person who sent him commanded him to do and say.
   He was the sender's stand-in. He was the sender's mouthpiece.

Consequently, an apostle was not an autonomous or independent person.

When Jesus called the Twelve His *apostles,* He used a word that was commonly known in the first century. It was not a word restricted to religious usage at all. A naval expedition sent by the king was called the king's apostle. A letter sent by an official was

14

called an apostle. A delegate of a high official was called an apostle. A ship that was sent out on a mission or an expedition could be called an apostle.

Jesus himself was called an apostle: "Therefore, holy brothers, who share in the heavenly calling, fix your thoughts on Jesus, the apostle and high priest whom we confess" (Hebrews 3:1).

How could Jesus be called an apostle?

1. He was an apostle because He was sent out on a mission by God. He was conceived of the Holy Spirit and the announcement that He was God's Son was made at His baptism. He was the one God anointed to be on a special mission, "God anointed Jesus of Nazareth with the Holy Spirit and power, and . . . he went around doing good and healing all who were under the power of the devil, because God was with him" (Acts 10:38).

2. While on that mission, Jesus spoke what His Father told Him to speak: "For I did not speak of my own accord, but the Father who sent me commanded me what to say and how to say it" (John 12:49).

3. Jesus did what His Father commanded Him to do: "By myself I can do nothing; I judge only as I hear, and my judgment is just, for I seek not to please myself but him who sent me" (John 5:30).

4. Consequently, Jesus represented God. To say He *represented* God literally means He re-presented God; He presented God again. This is the reason Jesus could say, "Anyone who has seen me has seen the Father" (John 14:9), and, "I and my Father are one" (John 10:30).

When the readers got a letter from Paul saying, "Paul, an apostle of Christ Jesus," they understood that this letter was not Paul's, but rather Christ's letter to them through Paul. Writing as an apostle, Paul was sensitive to the fact that he was writing divinely inspired words. They were not his. This is the message from Jesus and God.

That's the reason Christianity must be apostolic Christianity.

God has chosen to build the church on the foundation of the apostles and prophets, with Jesus Christ being the chief cornerstone (Ephesians 2:20). Christians rest their faith, belief, and practices upon what the apostles taught, for what they taught was God-taught. Paul affirmed that he spoke inspired words in 1 Corinthians 2:10-16.

The Sender

The Sender's Identification

Whom was Paul representing? Who was the higher authority? Paul identified his authority as Christ Jesus. *Jesus* is His name. The word *Christ* is His title. *Christ* is the Greek for *Messiah*.

Paul did not get to be an apostle of Jesus Christ by self-appointment. He became an apostle "by the command of God." Paul did not see two different sources here when he mentioned both Jesus and God. He linked the two up as a unit, as in many other places in the New Testament (John 1:1; 1 Timothy 1:16, 17; 6:14, 15; Colossians 2:9).

It is one thing to claim to be an apostle; it is another thing really to be one because of God's command. The word *command* comes from a Greek word that stresses the high rank of the person doing the commanding. It was a word used to refer to commands of kings and generals. No one gets any higher than God himself. God was the ultimate source, while Jesus was the immediate agent of Paul's apostleship.

The Sender's Functions

God is referred to as having two functions: "our Savior" (1 Timothy 1:1) and "the Father" (1 Timothy 1:2). Jesus Christ is also referred to as having two functions: "our hope" (1 Timothy 1:1) and "our Lord" (1 Timothy 1:2).

Notice the stress on the word *our*. God is not just for *me*, but for *us*. The song that talks about there being room for just two on the Jericho Road is wrong. There's never room for just two—Jesus and me. There is always room for Jesus, me, and anyone else in the world. The significance of the word *our* is the fact that every person in Christ shares the same status.

If God is "our Savior," then all of us are in the same state—lost. No one is superior or inferior to another. Paul develops that clearly in Romans (Romans 1:16; 2:9; 3:9, 22, 23; 10:12).

If God is the Father, then all of us in Christ belong to the same family. We are brothers and sisters to each other. Every one of us is a little child in a different stage of growth. Because He is Father, we can call Him "Abba," which means "Da Da" (Romans 8:15).

If Jesus is our hope, then all of us in Christ face the same situation in the future. We do not chart our own future. Our future is not because of *us*. *He* is our hope.

If Jesus is our Lord, then all of us in Christ are in the same status—servants under Him, for Him, and to Him. To see our God as Savior is to look *back* to the time when we were forgiven and to look *in* and know we are cleansed because of Him. To see Him as Lord is to look *up* and to look *inward,* understanding that we are His servants. To see Him as Father is to look *around,* for our Father is always with us. Our earthly fathers are with us via their sperma. And God the Father is with us because of the "sperma" that He has implanted within us who are in Christ (1 John 3:9). To see Him as our hope is to look *ahead.* Jesus promises that He will be with us *always* (Matthew 28:20; John 14:16, 18).

The word *Savior* is used in the Bible to refer both to God and to Jesus. It is used ten times in the pastorals. Six times it is used to refer to God the Father, and four times it is used to refer to the Son. How are both God and Jesus our Savior? God is the ultimate cause and Jesus is the immediate agent who made God's cause a reality. God planned it and Jesus executed it.

What are we saved from? The list is nearly endless. We are saved (1) from our sins, (2) from damnation, (3) from Hell, (4) from our own egos, (5) from loneliness, (6) from ourselves, (7) from a meaningless life, and (8) from our chief enemy, the devil.

Because God is our Savior, we are delivered from the negative. With Jesus as our hope, we are positioned in the positive. Jesus is our hope for the following:

1. For continual change into His likeness (2 Corinthians 3:18).
2. For eventually becoming just like Christ (1 John 3:2).
3. For resurrection and an inheritance (1 Peter 1:3, 4).
4. For protection (1 Peter 1:5).
5. For the Holy Spirit (John 14:16; Acts 2:38).
6. For answered prayers (John 14:13, 14).
7. For having all that Jesus is available to us (Ephesians 1:23; 3:19; 4:10).
8. For participation in the new world where God dwells (Revelation 21:1-4).

And the list goes on and on. Who is able to fathom this unspeakable gift?

Jesus does not just give us hope; He *is* our hope (Colossians 1:27). He is our live-in power of positive thinking. I am convinced that He affects the hemisphere of our brains that controls negative thinking. But we must practice the optimistic thinking. No wonder Paul wrote (in Philippians 4:8, 9 and Colossians 3:1, 2) that we are to set our minds on things that are above. We are to set our minds on Christ. We are to *think* Him and then *live* Him. As a person thinks within himself, so he is.

No wonder Paul was able to say that it was no longer he who lived, but Christ lived within him (Galatians 2:20). Since Jesus is our hope, we need to open up the rooms of our lives to Him so He can fill every chamber of our hearts with His presence.

God the Father and Christ the Lord have wrapped their relationship to us in the package of hope, grace, mercy, and peace. Sometimes we think of the word *lord* as a hardened dictator, but God has a tender heart for us.

"Grace, mercy, and peace" are more than just a greeting. They express a wish for Timothy's total well-being. And they are grounded in God and Jesus. *Grace* primarily refers to God's activity for us when we do not deserve it. It captures everything that God actively does or permits for our good. *Grace* is an action word in the Greek language; God is always active for our benefit. *Grace* is also a word that spotlights the fact that God cancels our debt. We even use that term today when we talk about a "grace" period for paying bills.

While *grace* could refer to God's motive for us, *mercy* can refer to His heartbeat for us. *Mercy* spotlights God's compassion and kindness when we need help. God's grace is beamed to us through His attitude of kindness for us.

Peace is the result of God's grace and mercy. *Peace* refers to the absence of alienation, the presence of security, and the state of a person who has a healthy relationship with God, himself, and others. It is a relational term.

God's grace is beamed to our badness. His mercy is beamed to our helplessness. His peace is beamed to our restlessness.

Although we do not deserve any of that, mankind is worth what God does for us. We are not worth it because of who we are; we are worth it because He has declared us worthy. We do not have to earn God's love and grace. That is the same way it is between parents and their children. When we bring new babies home from the hospital, those babies do not have to do one thing to earn our love. But they are worth it because they are ours, and we deem them worthy.

And that is the same way it is between God and us. God made us, and God does not make junk. God bought us through Jesus

Christ, and God does not buy junk. Jesus Christ is coming back for us and He is not coming back for the useless, worthless, good-for-nothing.

The Recipient

Paul wrote "to Timothy my true son in the faith" (1 Timothy 1:2). Paul repeatedly called Timothy his "son." (Note 1 Timothy 1:18; 2 Timothy 1:2; 1 Corinthians 4:17; Philippians 2:22.) The word *son* refers to somebody who has been lawfully begotten. Notice that Paul did not say that Timothy was his son biologically, but "in the faith"—that is, in Timothy's relationship to God through Jesus Christ. Timothy was Paul's son in the faith because Paul evidently evangelized Timothy. He then added Timothy to his traveling team and helped develop Timothy in spiritual maturity.

The father-son designation was an expression of endearment. Elsewhere, Paul said that he loved Timothy, and that he was faithful in the Lord (1 Corinthians 4:17); he gave Timothy credit "for carrying on the work of the Lord, just as I am" (1 Corinthians 16:10); he said that he had no one else like Timothy who took a genuine interest in others' welfare (Philippians 2:20); he spoke also of the fact that Timothy had proved himself (Philippians 2:22). Paul included Timothy in the opening of several of his letters (2 Corinthians, Philippians, Colossians, 1 Thessalonians, 2 Thessalonians and Philemon).

What a team! What congenial team members Paul and Timothy were to each other. They did not get caught in the trap that is so easy for many Christian team members to do. They did not start making comparisons, thinking about who was more significant. Comparisons lead to competition, which is followed by combative feelings and activities geared to canceling out one another.

Paul and Timothy are a mini-model of how people in the church should relate to one another—in unity, with encouragement, in harmony, with mutual respect, in spite of differences in personality, popularity, abilities, functions, and titles.

Once Jesus said, "By this all men will know that you are my disciples, if you love one another" (John 13:35). With that criterion, people could easily spot that Paul and Timothy were disciples of Jesus. May people be able to spot our discipleship by our love to others in God's family.

CHAPTER TWO

Watch Your Words

1 Timothy 1:3-7

The Problem Identified (1:3, 4)

Paul and Timothy had evidently been traveling together and arrived at Ephesus. Paul noted that there were some serious problems at the church at Ephesus; so he left Timothy there to deal with the problems while he himself went on to Macedonia.

When Paul left Timothy, he left him with encouraging, supporting words. We know that by Paul's choice of the word *urged*. That word comes from a Greek word that means to call someone alongside to hold that person up. So when Paul left Timothy, he left him with the kind of encouragement that a father would give to a son who was facing a discouraging situation. Paul reminds Timothy of his support—as it was in the past and will continue to be. There was no arrogance here on Paul's part. This is not an "I order you—now get with it." There is nothing here like a senior executive getting on the back of a junior assistant. Paul was probably writing about this task not to remind Timothy that he had to do it, but to help the church accept Timothy's ministry in these touchy areas.

Just what was the problem? It was twofold: an inappropriate talking and an inappropriate listening. "Command certain men not to teach false doctrines" (1 Timothy 1:3) was Paul's solution for the inappropriate talking. The next verse gives the solution for inappropriate listening: "nor to devote themselves to myths and endless genealogies."

Paul left Timothy so that Timothy would command certain men. The word for *command* was a word that was used for military orders in a life and death situation. The situation at Ephesus was indeed a life and death situation. If it continued, the people would find themselves with a shipwrecked faith (1 Timothy 1:19) and a departure from the faith (1 Timothy 6:21).

Not everybody in the church was caught up in this. Only "certain men" were involved. So Timothy was not to do his ministry of correction in shot-gun fashion. That would have been the easy way to tackle the problem of a few—bring it up to everybody, chew out everybody, command everybody—in the hopes that the guilty would catch the point. But Timothy's ministry was to be on a one-to-one basis. That takes more time, more relationship, more courage, and more patience.

We do not know who the "certain men" were. But they probably included Hymenaeus and Alexander (1 Timothy 1:20) and also one or two of the elders of the church. That is probably why Paul includes qualifications for elders in this letter. And it is why he includes in those qualifications that an elder must not be a recent convert, or become conceited, and be able to teach. Many of the qualifications of the elders in 1 Timothy 3 would prevent any of them from doing false teaching.

On an earlier occasion, Paul brought something to those elders' attention that was evidently now coming true. He said to them, "I know that after I leave, savage wolves will come in among you and will not spare the flock. Even from your own number men will arise and distort the truth in order to draw away disciples after them" (Acts 20:29, 30).

These "certain men" were teaching "false doctrines." The words *to teach false doctrines* are all one word in the Greek. It is a word that means to teach something entirely different. What kind of teaching would that be—teaching that would be so different from the truth as to cause a life and death situation? We get a clear indication of what it was from Galatians 1:6-9 and 3:1-5. Clearly, it was a teaching that took one's eyes off of Jesus and introduced another way to be saved—that bypassed the crucified and risen Lord. It seems clear through the rest of 1 Timothy that the false doctrine was related to Judaizers, those who taught that a person had to become a Jew in order to be saved, regardless of his relationship to Jesus.

Paul wrote this warning for the protection of both the speakers and the hearers. If the speakers didn't quit, they would be accursed (Galatians 1:8). If the hearers "bought into it," they would be led astray (2 Corinthians 11:2-4).

Although verse 3 deals with inappropriate teaching, verse 4 deals with inappropriate listening. What these people were listening to—"myths and endless genealogies"—was no doubt the

Hearers have A Respon. Too.

"false doctrines" that were being taught (verse 3). The false doctrines were coming in the attractive package of myths and genealogies.

The words *devote themselves to* is translated by other writers as "pay attention to," "give heed to," "occupy their minds with." The Greek word does not refer to casual listening but rather "an attaching oneself to" what is heard. It means to accept and affirm it, and then be committed to it. However, getting attached to a different doctrine begins by casual listening. No Christian has the liberty to sit at the feet of just anyone and listen to just anything. It can too easily become what we accept.

What would cause some people who are in Christ to begin to teach a doctrine so different that it would jeopardize the salvation of their hearers? There are many possible motivations, but two are apparent in this situation. One is the desire of a teacher to have disciples follow him. There is an attractiveness to having people dependent upon you. As Paul had warned the Ephesian elders this would happen (Acts 20:30), so here in this situation it seems to have come to be.

A second motivation is the desire for financial benefit. When people begin to follow your teaching, they will often back that up by monetary support. That is no doubt why Paul wrote that "the love of money is a root of all kinds of evil. Some people, eager for money, have wandered from the faith and pierced themselves with many griefs" (1 Timothy 6:10). Why did Paul include that in this letter? Probably because some of those teaching false doctrines were doing it for what they would gain monetarily. That is probably also the reason Paul mentioned that an elder should not be a "lover of money" (1 Timothy 3:3). Once a person has a following of people that is backed up with the support of their purses, it is extremely difficult to quit the teaching that produced that following, even though the teacher may come to know that what he is teaching is wrong. It is super tough to admit you have been wrong when your popularity and financial security have been built upon being wrong.

We understand the motivations of the false teachers. We see the error in them, but still we understand them. We know they believe they have something to gain. But what about their listeners? What do they have to gain? What causes some people to be lured to false teaching? What caused it in Timothy's day, and what causes it today? Let me suggest briefly several reasons:

1. An inadequate introduction to true teaching.
2. An outstanding orator. Some people whose content is wrong are outstanding in the skill of communication; while others who have the right content are less than effective in their methods of communication. The result is that people follow the false teachers instead of the true.
3. The lure of the novel. Some people are attracted to anything that is new.
4. The lure of interesting theories that capture their thinking.
5. The magnetism of being loved. Some who teach false doctrine make their hearers feel loved, important, and needed. It is tough to reject a person's teaching if that person is warm, kind, gentle, and outgoing. (Teachers of truth should take a lesson here.)
6. The false teaching may be surrounded by the best equipment available—audio-visual, musical, and the works. All of that has an attractiveness to it. How can something be wrong if it is so first-class?
7. The attractiveness that some of the funds collected will be used for good causes that touch the heart. Income to support false teaching can be multiplied when some of those funds are marketed as being used to build orphanages, to feed the starving, or for some other noble cause.

Anyone is vulnerable to cave in to false teaching. Even Timothy was vulnerable. That is why Paul wrote to Timothy,

> But as for you, continue in what you have learned and have become convinced of, because you know those from whom you learned it, and how from infancy you have known the holy Scriptures, which are able to make you wise for salvation through faith in Christ Jesus. All Scripture is God-breathed and is useful for teaching, rebuking, correcting and training in righteousness, so that the man of God may be thoroughly equipped for every good work (2 Timothy 3:14-17).

Paul advised Timothy to do the following to keep from caving in. It's good advice for anyone today, too.
1. Don't be so quick to turn away from what you were taught.
2. Be able to trust the teachers fully.
3. Know the Scriptures.
4. Depend upon the Scriptures to equip you for every good work.

Paying attention to "myths and endless genealogies" was hurting the church at Ephesus. *Myths* literally means plans conceived in the mind. It denotes teaching that is calculated to please the ear rather than to speak the truth. Myths were untrue stories that came out of someone's imagination. Myths existed in both the Greek and the Jewish world. The myths here are probably connected with the "endless genealogies"—which were Jewish in origin. Titus 1:14 cautions against "Jewish myths." The Jews were experts in creating myths and fables that were designed to make Judaism look superior to any other system. This was particularly prevalent in the Intertestamental period.

The "endless genealogies" were probably also Jewish in nature. The Jews loved to trace their genealogies and make a case for being in the right family and being connected to the right individuals in the past. This can be endless. For some, once it gets started, there is no stopping—they get hooked on it. One not only traces his own genealogy, but his immediate family, his relatives, and others.

While myths were designed to make Judaism look superior, endless genealogies were traced to make an individual have higher status than others. The Jews wanted their status to be linked to genealogies; even Paul referred to his past genealogy when he said, "If anyone else thinks he has reasons to put confidence in the flesh, I have more: circumcised on the eighth day, of the people of Israel, of the tribe of Benjamin, a Hebrew of Hebrews; in regard to the law, a Pharisee" (Philippians 3:4, 5). But look at what Paul also said, "Whatever was to my profit I now consider loss for the sake of Christ" (Philippians 3:7).

Some people suggest that the "endless genealogies" refer to Gnosticism, which was a Greek pagan philosophy. However, Gnosticism as a system had not been developed this early, and there is no evidence that the Gnostics ever used the word *genealogy* to refer to their system.

Some Gentiles who came into Christianity might also have begun tracing their genealogies, seeking status. Greeks did indeed tie their status to their ancestry; some of them, including Alexander the Great, even created false genealogies to enhance their positions.

It was wise of Paul not to be specific about the content of the myths and endless genealogies, lest we believe that those particular ones would have been the only ones to avoid. Whatever it is that leads us away from Christ and into "controversies" rather than to God's Word is to be avoided.

It is possible to hear such talk in home Bible studies and Sunday-school class discussions—speculations that are not tied to reality, which could be equated with "meaningless talk." The word controversies is translated in other versions as "speculations." The root idea does spotlight quarrels, disputes, arguments, and strife. People with differing opinions began to promote their ideas over those of others. That is probably why Paul said that elders should not be quarrelsome (1 Timothy 3:3). He also said that a leader like Timothy should not

> have anything to do with foolish and stupid arguments, because you know they produce quarrels. And the Lord's servant must not quarrel; instead, he must be kind to everyone, able to teach, not resentful. Those who oppose him he must gently instruct, in the hope that God will grant them repentance leading them to a knowledge of the truth (2 Timothy 2:23-25).

The kind of speculations that give rise to arguments turn our attention inward instead of upward and outward. Consequently, they do not promote God's work. The term God's *work* is translated by other writers as God's "stewardship," God's "administration," or the divine "plan." The Greek word is related, in function, to the idea of "building up." But just what is God building up in His divine plan? What is it that God was intending to administrate through His strategy? The same Greek word was used in Ephesians 1:10, where it clearly identifies God's work or plan as being unity among people. The rest of Ephesians develops clearly that God's plan was to bring all people together into one family. God's plan was to include people. But Judaism, by using its myths and never-ending pedigrees, excluded people who couldn't fit into the record of ancestry.

God's divine plan of bringing people into unity under one head—Christ—is a plan that is entered into by faith. That is why Paul says that God's work "is by faith." It is not a unity that exists because we all have the right answers. It is not a unity that depends on our conformity to the same opinions. It is a unity that exists because we are *in* Christ. We must be big enough to say, "I don't know." We must be big enough to include someone else as a brother or sister in Christ who may have a different opinion from ours. That was what Paul was getting at when he said, "Accept him whose faith is weak, without passing judgment on disputable matters" (Romans 14:1). That is also what Paul was including when he wrote that his prayer was for us to be "rooted and established in love," and that we know "how wide and long and high and deep is the love of Christ" (Ephesians 3:17, 18).

There are several difficulties that come as we begin to listen, even casually, to false teaching that gives rise to speculations. Some of those follow:

1. Truth gets mixed up with error, and it becomes hard to tell when one ends and the other begins.
2. What we pay attention to, we eventually become.
3. The more we hear it, the more we and others believe it. This is the principle of reinforcement.
4. Eventually, we accept error as truth without challenging it.
5. We can easily make it our goal to convert people to a system or to a position rather than to the Savior—the person of Christ.
6. We get hooked on mental aerobics. That is, we just love to dabble in mental gymnastics simply for the sake of mental exercise.
7. We become more interested in being creative than in being new creatures.
8. We become more interested in words of discussion than in actions of love.
9. We become more interested in arguments than in *agape*.
10. We may want to be seen as superior rather than as servants.
11. It is easy as we begin to major in speculations and arguments to allow our heads to grow larger than our hearts.
12. We become dogmatic without knowledge.
13. We become moralists who begin to judge others by our standards and our mental abilities.
14. We reject others rather than accept others.
15. Our consciences become seared.
16. We become conceited.
17. We begin to love friction and difficulties (1 Timothy 6:4, 5).

The Goal of Christian Teaching (1:5)

The goal of Christian teaching is "love, which comes from a pure heart and a good conscience and a sincere faith" (1 Timothy

1:5). The bulls-eye of any Christian instruction should be that it produce love. And any teaching that does not do that hinders God's intention for His church.

But love is not enough—it must come from the right kind of person. That person is described as someone with a pure heart, good conscience, and sincere faith. The words *pure heart* spotlight proper motivation. The person with a pure heart has no ulterior motives. He is not trying to show how clever he is, or trying to get rich off of his teaching, or trying to draw disciples after him, or trying to show others how wrong they are. His only desire is to enhance the unity of God's people in Christ and to bring them to maturity.

A *good conscience* spotlights what a person thinks. The word *conscience* literally means "a knowing with." A person with a good conscience is one who "knows with" God; that is, he evaluates what he knows on the basis of God's knowledge. He also "knows with" himself; that is, what he is speaking he knows within himself squares with what he himself really believes. He is not knowing one thing and creating something else in order to be seen as a creative genius.

The *sincere faith* spotlights what a person believes. Sincerity is the opposite of hypocrisy. It points out genuineness. The sincere person is not saying one thing and living out another.

Out of the right kind of person must come the right kind of action: love, *agape* -style. This kind of love is other-oriented. It seeks out the needs of others and moves to meet those needs, not considering what self will get out of it. Elsewhere, the Scriptures make it clear that that kind of love is a goal that God has for all of us:

> A new command I give you: Love one another. As I have loved you, so you must love one another. By this all men will know that you are my disciples, if you love one another (John 13:34, 35)

> Jesus replied: "'Love the Lord your God with all your heart and with all your soul and with all your mind.' This is the first and greatest commandment. And the second is like it: 'Love your neighbor as yourself'" (Matthew 22:37, 38).

> Let no debt remain outstanding, except the continuing debt to love one another, for he who loves his fellowman has fulfilled the law.

The commandments, "Do not commit adultery," "Do not murder," "Do not steal," "Do not covet," and whatever other commandment there may be, are summed up in this one rule: "Love your neighbor as yourself." Love does no harm to its neighbor. Therefore love is the fulfillment of the law (Romans 13:8-10).

And now these three remain: faith, hope and love. But the greatest of these is love (1 Corinthians 13:13).

You, my brothers, were called to be free. But do not use your freedom to indulge your sinful nature; rather, serve one another in love. The entire law is summed up in a single command: "Love your neighbor as yourself" (Galatians 5:13, 14).

The question is not how much we know, but how well do we love? It's not just what is in our head, but also what is in our heart? It is not how many disciples do we have attached to *us,* but how many people are we serving? It is not how many people turn to *us* for their answers, but how many people do we turn toward to meet their needs?

The Detour of False Teaching (1:6, 7)

Getting hooked on controversies causes one to get more involved in loathing than in loving. Pure hearts become polluted. Good consciences become seared, and sincere faith becomes insincere. Instead of reaching out to meet the needs of others, there is specialization in meaningless talk.

It is usually a gradual digression. That is expressed by the words *wandered away.* They probably never intended to get off the track. They just gradually began to sway, to swerve, to step aside—and finally missed the mark. One translator puts it this way: "Such people have missed this whole idea." Yes, how easy it is to miss the idea that God wants us to live in unity with love for others in His family in spite of their differences.

Notice that paying attention to false teachings is the first step to wandering, straying, swerving, stepping aside, and missing God's whole idea. It isn't that the person is doing anything outwardly immoral; he is just engaging meaningless talk. Other translators say, "empty talk," "fruitless talking," "wilderness of words," "vain babbling," "purposeless talk," "empty reasoning," "fruitless discussion," and "high-flown gobbledygook."

The initial motive of these people was good; however, not everybody should want to be a teacher. James said, "Not many of you should presume to be teachers, my brothers, because you know that we who teach will be judged more strictly" (James 3:1). The teacher has an awesome responsibility, for the product of what he teaches may mean eternal life or eternal death to his hearers. While the motives were good, the credentials were bad— "they do not know what they are talking about or what they so confidently affirm" (1 Timothy 1:7). Sometimes we may fail to realize the meaning of our own words; we may teach what we do not fully understand. The danger is that when we become very confident in what we are saying, we are not open to hear and understand the truth. We need to take the position, "This is where I am on this issue today, but I am open. I may not have this same opinion next year, for I will continue to study and allow God's Word, God's people, and God's Spirit to impact my thinking."

Some people have certain topics upon which they harp and have closed the door of their minds to any further insight. That feeds and encourages conceit. Later, Paul wrote that such a person is "conceited and understands nothing" (1 Timothy 6:4).

If Timothy's mission of making these kind of corrections was to succeed, it would take the backing of good leaders in the church. That is probably one reason Paul included the qualifications of elders and deacons in this letter. Those men must not become "conceited." If the qualifications of the leaders could be watered down, the teachers of that church could continue to get away with what they were doing.

Each of us needs to be cautious against dreaming up theories for which we have no clear Biblical teaching and then attracting people to those theories. We must all ask, "Where is this kind of teaching leading? Will it really help people to grow into Christlikeness? Or is it simply another activity in mental gymnastics? Will it help people to have pure hearts, good consciences, and sincere faith—and out of that to love others? Or will it detour, detract, swerve, or sway people from the central thrust of Christianity—unity amid diversity, and love for others?"

We must also be cautious lest we repeat a certain idea or theory so often that we become so confident in it that our heads become bigger than our hearts. If we want to be teachers, then we must teach in a way that love can come out of people's lives because they have heard and seen the Spirit of Christ shine through us.

CHAPTER THREE

Law or Grace

1 Timothy 1:8-20

The Purpose of Law (1:8-11)

Those who were wanting to be teachers of the law were evidently misusing the law because they had not understood its intention. The "law" Paul mentioned here referred to the old written code, the Old Covenant, the sacred writings of the Old Testament. It also referred to the "oral law" designed by the Pharisees. These teachers of the law were probably pushing the superiority of Judaism through myths and genealogies.

The intention of the law, however, was to bring people to Christ. "The law was put in charge to lead us to Christ that we might be justified by faith. Now that faith has come, we are no longer under the supervision of the law" (Galatians 3:24, 25).

The practical carrying out of the intentions of the law is done when people properly love God and love one another. This is spotlighted in Matthew 7:12; 22:36-40; Romans 13:8-10.

God originally created man in His own image. But man sinned and fell short of the glory of God so that soon every thought of mankind was fixed on just one thing—evil—all the time (Genesis 6:5). That means man had severed his relational skills to get along with others properly. Instead of reconciliation, there was revenge. Instead of unity, there was disunity. Instead of peace, there was war. Man was so committed to living life his own way that God established the law to give man guidelines about how to treat God and others properly.

Since the purpose of the law was to bring us to Christ, and since the practical application of the law is done through love, any teaching that strays from Christ and love violates the intention of the law.

Many people who taught the legalism of the law were more interested in "law" than in "love." They failed to understand

31

what the law could *not* do. The law could not heal the inner person. The law could not give the divine life to live out the intentions of the law (Galatians 3:21). That divine life is the Holy Spirit, the fruit of which is listed in Galatians 5:22-25.

The law was good but limited. Indeed, the law was good in that it pointed people to the Messiah and kept people hemmed in, held in a kind of life-style that prevented them from destroying each other until the divine Holy Spirit was available to live in the inner person and change us from the inside out.

That is why the law is called "good" (1 Timothy 1:8). But that is also why it was not made for "good men." Good men are those who have been made righteous by having faith in Jesus Christ, having their sins forgiven, and having received the Holy Spirit. The word translated "good" is literally the Greek word for "righteous." A person is made righteous in Christ, "God made him who had no sin to be sin for us, so that in him we might become the righteousness of God" (2 Corinthians 5:21). A "righteous" person is not someone who is perfect, but someone who has received both acquittal and equipment. He has been acquitted of his sins by forgiveness and has been equipped for a new kind of life by the Holy Spirit.

The law is not in competition against the gospel, as some people have suggested. The law pointed to the Messiah, and the gospel revealed the Messiah. The law kept people hemmed in to respecting each others' rights by the restrictions of the law. The gospel gives a person a new inner life to live in reconciliation with others.

The law is for the unrighteous. But why? Because the law does the following:

1. It points out what sin is (Romans 3:20; 7:7, 8).
2. It keeps people hemmed in, keeps people from destroying one another.
3. It instructs the conscience (Romans 7). It was because of the law that some people could feel guilty when they had mistreated others and had neglected God.

Does this mean that the Christian has no law at all? Of course not. But we do not have a law of legalism; it is the law of liberty (James 1:25; 2:12). That law of liberty frees us from the legalism of the Old Covenant. That is because in Christ we have received the Holy Spirit, who equips us from the inside to do the intentions of the law (2 Corinthians 3:17, 18). That means we are now free to become what God intends for us to be. We are liberated to become

Christlike because His type of life now lives inside of us. The law that controls us is the "royal law" of love (James 2:8). This "royal law" serves others; it does not sever through condemnation:

> You, my brothers, were called to be free. But do not use your freedom to indulge the sinful nature; rather, serve one another in love. The entire law is summed up in a single command: "Love your neighbor as yourself" (Galatians 5:13, 14).

So the old law was written for those who did not have the divine inner life that would equip them to live properly with God and with others. Paul listed some of the expressions of people who do not live well with others (1 Timothy 1:9, 10). These are the non-lovers. They do not have the "royal law" of love living inside of them through the Holy Spirit. They are not freed to love the way God is love, because they are enslaved to sin. Consequently, the purpose of the law for them is to give them some guidelines about how to live with one another, but these guidelines are restrictive and legalistic. A person cannot carry them out even though he does want to, but the Christian who has God's Spirit carries out God's kind of love because he wants to—not because he has to.

Who are those non-lovers?

1. Lawbreakers—those who ignore God's law. They live as if there is no law. They may know the law, but refuse to do it.
2. Rebels—those who will not submit to authority. They may recognize law, but they refuse to live under it.
3. The ungodly—these are not only indifferent, but are actively defiant against God. They have no respect for God as a Person or as God.
4. Sinful—these have no moral standards. No wonder they need a law.
5. The unholy and irreligious—these are thoroughly secular. They have caved in to the culture of their time; and, consequently, they will purposely trample on anything sacred.
6. Those who kill their fathers or mothers—these are those who have both bodily killed their parents and who have killed them emotionally because of their ungratefulness and lack of respect.
7. Murderers—these are killers of people.
8. Adulterers—the literal Greek is not the word for "adulterers," but for anyone who is sexually perverted.

33

9. Perverts—this word in the Greek spotlights homosexuality.
10. Slave traders—literally refers to "men stealers." This can be translated "kidnappers." Today many children are being kidnapped for sex. That is one way of being a "slave trader."
11. Liars—these are those who have no regard for integrity.
12. Perjurers—these are those who break oaths. They usually do so for monetary gain.

All of the above expressions idicate followers of ideas that are "contrary to ... sound doctrine" (1 Timothy 1:10). The word for *sound* is a word that emphasizes healing. The non-loving actions above bring disease into people's spirits rather than healing. Christ brings healing to the inner person by His activity on the cross: "But he was pierced through for our transgressions, he was crushed for our iniquities; the punishment that brought us peace was upon him, and by his wounds we are healed" (Isaiah 53:5). The teaching that brings inner healing upholds "the glorious gospel" (1 Timothy 1:11). It is not the teaching that conforms to the legalistic condemnations of the law.

Is there any hope for the kinds of people that Paul listed? Of course there is. There is hope *if* the law is used properly—that is, used to bring people to Christ, not to judge people after they have come to the Messiah.

In the next section, Paul lifted up himself as a tangible example of God's available grace. Paul showed the extent of God's forgiveness and how He can use a person despite his past.

The Reality of Grace (1:12-20)

Paul illustrated what the gospel would do that the law could not do. In Christ, Paul received the following:
1. Strength—God never calls us to do something He will not help us to do.
2. A consideration of faithfulness—even though a person has had a bad past, *in* Christ God considers a person to be available and potentially dependable.
3. A ministry—God does not keep holding our past against us when we are in Christ; He puts us into service.
4. Mercy—God understands where we have come from. In Christ is mercy that is beyond our past.
5. Abundant grace—God's grace is always greater than man's disgrace.
6. New life-style—this is seen in the words *faith* and *love*.

34

Paul made it clear that even though a person has lived a rotten life, God's grace and mercy are greater. God's desire to use us is greater than man's past experience of abusing God. The law points us to Christ, so that in Christ our whole past can be obliterated.

Many people need the truth about God's relationship to Paul. Paul was a "blasphemer and a persecutor and a violent man" (1 Timothy 1:13); yet notice the change that took place in his life. Many people have locked themselves up into their past blunders. Many people are paralyzed by their past life-styles. Many people have become concreted to the yesterdays of their lives, but God wants to give them the new law of liberty, which frees them from the paralysis of their past. There is hope; there is new birth; there is a new spirit; there is transformation. There is continual change awaiting those who will surrender to Christ.

The law brings guilt; the gospel brings forgiveness. The law points out our meanness; the gospel points out God's mercy. The law condemns; the gospel saves.

Isn't it time for the church to celebrate God's provision for the sinners? Isn't it time for the church to accept the forgiveness of God and forget the bitter past? Someone has suggested that the church is the only army that shoots its own wounded. We must be willing to forgive ourselves and others as God does. We will do that only if we understand that we now live by the law of liberty, which is the royal law of love. We do not have to keep dumping God's old law onto people and remind them of their past guilt. We need to assure people continually that they are forgiven in Christ.

Many do not live the new life they have in Christ because they are not sure they really have it. But celebrating the assurance of it can cause people to leave the worship service more determined to live in a Christlike way because of gratitude and respect to God, who considers us faithful, who forgives us, who shows mercy, and whose grace is abundant to us despite our past.

Paul set himself up as a pattern of what God was willing to do for *everyone*. Jesus Christ came into the world to save sinners. And Paul confessed, "I am the worst." But even for the worst, Christ gave mercy (1 Timothy 1:13) and unlimited patience (1 Timothy 1:16). The word translated "patience" here stresses putting up with difficult people. Paul had been a difficult person: he was "blasphemer"; he denied that Jesus was the Messiah. He was a "persecutor"; he tried to destroy the work of God's church. He

35

was a "violent man"; he dragged both men and women out of houses to take them to trial with the intention that they would be executed. But God knows how to put up with difficult people.

Paul was an example for *everyone*. The word *example* (1 Timothy 1:16) literally means that he was an "under-type." He was the type or pattern under which every sinner can stand. If God forgave Paul and could use him in meaningful service, anyone could be forgiven and used. If anyone believes he is beyond the scope of God's circle of love, he should look at the conversion of Paul. The reality of it does not rest on the significance of the sinners but on the magnificence of our Lord.

Thus, Paul broke out into a sentence of praise and celebration to Jesus, "Now to the King eternal, immortal, invisible, the only God, be honor and glory for ever and ever. Amen" (1 Timothy 1:17). His celebration of God's greatness should be ours.

1. The King eternal (literally, "the King of the ages"). That means that Jesus is the Lord of the past, the present, and future.

2. Immortal. He will never wear out, wear down, or be destroyed. The second law of thermodynamics does not apply to God. Time does not cause Him to deteriorate.

3. Invisible—He is not restricted to our time/space dimensions. He is not physical or material. He makes himself known, but He cannot be seen, captured, or manhandled.

4. The only God. He is unique. He is one of a kind. There is no other beside Him. In fact, other gods really do not exist, even though man has created many in his own image.

Our response to the only God should be "honor and glory." Giving Him honor means giving Him all the respect He deserves. Giving Him glory is to characterize Him through our thoughts and life-styles. God's glory is God's character, and the way to glorify Him is to characterize Him so His presence can be felt.

How are we honoring and glorifying God? Is He getting the proper credit? Is He getting the proper respect? Is He getting appreciation? Are we giving Him attention? Are we manifesting His inner life-style? If we turn our eyes off of Jesus and turn them onto the legalism with the nitpicking, the criticism, the pressing of opinions onto others concerning myths and genealogies, then we will be vulnerable to detouring from Christlikeness. Every Christian is vulnerable to that; that is why Paul instructed Timothy to tell people to quit teaching the strange doctrines and others to quit listening to them.

The fact that every Christian is vulnerable is seen in Paul's caution to Timothy in what follows (1 Timothy 1:18ff). Paul mentioned some prophecies once made about Timothy. The content of those prophecies we do not know, but the purpose we do know; "by following them you may fight the good fight" (1 Timothy 1:18). Evidently, prophets were at Timothy's ordination and had declared that Timothy was to give his life to fighting the good fight.

To understand this "good fight," let us consider for a moment its opposite, a "bad" fight. What would be a bad fight? Here are some elements of a bad fight:

1. Following the wrong commander in chief. Our commander in chief is Jesus.
2. Fighting our own buddies instead of the enemy. Christians do this as they go after the jugular vein of other Christians who have different opinions.
3. Becoming deserters to the cause.
4. Refusing to allow others (particularly those who were once outsiders) to enlist in the ranks.
5. Failing to build up the rest of the members with encouragement and support.
6. Failing to select properly equipped leaders.
7. Failing to keep the faith.
8. Disregarding our good conscience as we go chasing "projects."
9. Using wrong tactics.
10. Failing to praise our Commander in Chief, Jesus.
11. Using the wrong weapons. (See Ephesians 6:10-18.)
12. Failing to use the right weapons.

While Paul was an illustration of what God can do for people who have formerly been on the wrong side, he pointed out Hymenaeus and Alexander as examples of what can happen to people who do not commit themselves to fight the good fight. They are probably two people who were magnetized by myths and endless genealogies and wanted to teach others the strange doctrines and creative novelties.

To deliver them over to Satan was to disfellowship them from the church. This was done to lead them to repentance. It was isolation from God's people that would leave them in the world without the support and encouragement of God's family. It was to be a foretaste of what life in Hell is like. Because the fellowship, support, love, and acceptance are so essential to Christians in the church, the disengagement from that can bring a person to repentance.

This disfellowshiping is to protect the guilty parties who are bringing disruption and seeking to lead the church astray as well as to protect the church itself. On another occasion, Paul advised a church to disfellowship a member for the purpose of bringing him to repentance and to preserve the church (1 Corinthians 5). That individual did repent and was restored to the fellowship (2 Corinthians 1).

Probably, all of us who are parents know something about that kind of discipline. It happens when we send our children to their rooms, where they have no contact with others. Ordered isolation can be an effective form of discipline.

Elsewhere Paul wrote to reject a divisive man after a first and second warning (Titus 3:10). That was in the same type of context as this instance. Divisive people were involved in controversies, genealogies, strife, and disputes about the law, which were unprofitable and worthless (Titus 3:9). That kind of teaching turns people against each other and destroys unity.

God's plan is to bring people into unity under Christ. That is God's wisdom. When we use our human wisdom to detour people from unity to disunity, from peace to animosity, from acceptance to condemnation, from eternal life to endless genealogies, from the Master to myths, from salvation to speculation, from fruitful discipleship to fruitless discussion—we are undoing what Christ came to do. People who have that mind-set bring enough destruction to themselves and to others that their destruction is called "shipwreck" (1 Timothy 1:19) and is worthy of isolation until a change occurs.

The change that is to occur is a change toward more Christlikeness. When that change happens, then we must reaffirm our love and fellowship to such people (2 Corinthians 2).

Let us help each other stay on track. May our ship reach harbor and not get destroyed on the rocks. May the salvation we have in Christ not be torpedoed by the speculations we have in our heads.

CHAPTER FOUR

The Priority of Prayer

1 Timothy 2:1-8

When Paul wrote, "First of all," he was saying that this is priority stuff. The church at Ephesus needed to hear that, as does the church today. It is so easy to let everything else take priority, and then bring prayer in when the activities are not working well.

That is what was happening in the church at Ephesus. They were making their communication with one another the priority. They were emphasizing teaching and learning (1 Timothy 1:3-7). And don't we do the same today?

1. Compare the number of people who will come for a preaching service over against those who would come for a prayer meeting.
2. Compare the amount of time we actually pray at a mid-week prayer meeting over against the time teaching is being done. Isn't it true that to get people out for a prayer meeting, we have to have something else on the program to lure them?
3. Compare the amount of time we spend preparing for a Sunday-school lesson or sermon over against the time we spend in prayer about it.
4. Compare the amount of time we spend trying to convince someone his doctrine is somewhat erroneous over against the time we will pray for that individual.

Is it possible that one of the reasons the church at Ephesus was in such difficulty is that they had put their prayer life on the shelf?

Our lives are so crowded. If the church is an involved church, its calendar is crowded. We may not intend for it to happen, but gradually, prayer time gets squeezed out of the schedule.

That was about to happen in the life of the early church. The church in Jerusalem had grown significantly. Some estimate that by Acts 6, the membership in Jerusalem was over 20,000. More people means more people with needs to be met. One of those needs was the need for daily food, and the church had been taking care of that need. But some were complaining that they were being neglected. The apostles realized their lives were being crowded with many meaningful and necessary activities—so crowded that their priorities were being misplaced. They asked the congregation to select other people who could involve themselves in the meaningful ministry of the distribution of food.

Then the apostles said, "[We] will give our attention to prayer and the ministry of the word" (Acts 6:4). Notice the order—prayer is listed first.

The word translated "then" (1 Timothy 2:1) is the Greek word for "therefore." Anytime we see that word, we need to look into the rear view mirror and investigate what has just been said. Paul had just finished talking about some people who had shipwrecked their faith (he mentioned two men, 1 Timothy 1:19, 20). He moved immediately without a break, using the word *then (therefore)*, to make it clear that part of the problem of those who had shipwrecked their faith was a weak prayer life.

Instead of praying for one another, we too often begin to prey upon each other.

All Kinds of Prayer (2:1)

Prayer is communication with God. But there are many different kinds of prayers, as there are many different kinds of ways to communicate with someone. We can congratulate, scold, question, praise, share our innermost thoughts, share events going on in our lives, request favors, and communicate in many more ways. And so it is in our communication with God.

Communication literally means the process of coming into common oneness. Communication helps us draw into a common oneness with those with whom we are communicating if that communication is on a positive note. Our communication with God should help us draw closer to Him.

Paul mentioned four different kinds of prayers—"requests, prayers, intercession and thanksgiving" (1 Timothy 2:1). The word for *requests* is a word that emphasizes "begging someone on the behalf of another." The requests could be made to God or another human being. In this context, Paul was referring to our asking God to help other people. But the Greek word can literally mean asking *any* person to help. It may be in the midst of our asking God that He opens up our minds and hearts to remember someone else who could be a resource in that situation. Then we have the responsibility to go to that person and ask for help. The point is that we should be willing to go to bat for another person's need, regardless of where we have to go in order to do so.

The Greek for *prayers* is a word that is reserved for addressing God with any kind of prayer. There is a kind of help that only God can supply. We need to go to the throne of God with that request.

Intercession is an extremely interesting Greek word and is used in many different ways in both the Old and New Testaments. It is only when we see all the different shades of this word and put them together that we can catch the full impact of the significance of intercession. Here are some of the meanings of that word:

1. To meet or approach.
2. A happening—to light upon a situation without intending to.
3. To reach toward—it was used of territories that would stretch to the farthest limit of their boundaries.
4. To fall upon—this usage referred to people who responded to the king's orders to "fall upon" enemies for the purpose of destroying them.
5. An appeal.

Let's put all of these together. To make intercession is to *meet* or *approach* God on the behalf of another. It is for those people or situations that we just light upon—come across without intending to. That refers to those happenchance situations. As Christians, we should take advantage of the opportunities such situations offer. For instance, we might light upon an accident, and use that opportunity to pray an intercessory prayer for the people involved. We might happen upon a child who looks lonely and unkept. Do we just go by without anything burning in our hearts? That is a time to make intercessory prayer for that child.

There will be many times in your life that a person's name or situation will just pop into your mind. Immediately you should go to God in intercessory prayer for that person.

Our intercessory prayer involves a spiritual battle. "Our struggle is not against flesh and blood, but against the rulers, against the authorities, against the powers of this dark world and against the spiritual forces of evil in heavenly realms" (Ephesians 6:12). We are in a cosmic spiritual battle. The apostle Paul listed the armor we are to use: truth, righteousness, the gospel of peace, faith, salvation, the Word of God (Ephesians 6:13-17). Many people stop reading after verse 17, but that armor includes verse 18, "And pray in the Spirit on all occasions with all kinds of prayers and requests. With this in mind, be alert and always keep on praying for all the saints." We are to use intercessory prayer to fall upon the enemy. And the enemy is the devil. We are to fight with the weapon of prayer. We are to ask God's ruling power to invade what is going on on this earth.

God has set boundaries for us. And His boundaries are indeed large boundaries. He has given us tremendous potential. The devil has caused some people to be committed to "impossibility thinking." That needs to be changed, and it can be changed with intercessory prayer.

Intercessory prayer is to meet God on the behalf of other people—even those whom we do not know but happen to come across our way. It is to be used to help stretch the potential that God has given to people. It is to fall upon the spiritual enemy, the devil, and chase him back with the power of prayer that summons the presence of God.

Do we know how to pray for another person? Do we know all that is going on so that what we say is the content of the prayer that is needed? Of course not. Admitting that is no problem, for we are admitting our own limitations. Thus we pray with the assistance of the Holy Spirit.

One of the places that the word *intercession* is used is in Romans 8:26: "In the same way, the Spirit helps us in our weakness. We do not know what we ought to pray for, but the Spirit himself intercedes for us with groans that words cannot express." When we read that the Spirit "helps us," it means literally in the Greek that the Holy Spirit will "take ahold with us" in this situation. The Spirit comes to help in our weakness. He makes intercession on our behalf. There are many times that we do not know what to say, such as in a time of oppression, disappointment, depression, tragedy, conflict, or sufferings that others go through. Our own spirits are in deep distress; we want to do something, but many times our first reaction is just to sigh, groan, or gasp. We may do it verbally, or there may be that inner feeling—"I want to do something. I am greatly affected, but I don't know what to do." It is at that time that the Holy Spirit will take those sighs, groans, and gasps and intercede to the Father for us with groans (our groans) that words (our words) could not express. We are finite. We are weak. Some situations and feelings are beyond our words, but the Holy Spirit understands and goes to the Father with the appropriate expressions. The Holy Spirit acts in our place. He becomes our pray-er. There are many times that we ought to ask the Holy Spirit to pray for us, not as an escape from our praying, but to join us in praying with words and understandings beyond our present knowledge.

Let's live lives of intercessory prayer—being open, realizing that many things may not be by "chance." Perhaps God links us up so that we can be intercessors for others. That includes people we do not know, and people with whom we may not agree.

Thanksgivings means giving appreciation. It means to be filled with gratitude and to express it to God. Giving real thanksgiving to God is one of the toughest things for people in the western culture to do. That is because we have been trained to idolize our independence and our own abilities. To give thanks is to admit that whatever has happened is because someone else has provided and done things for us. That hurts our egos. To give thanks is to admit that we are recipients, not the initiators. Our egos must give way again. To give thanks is to admit that someone else is the benefactor and the cause. So long, ego! To give thanks is to become humble. To give thanks is to recognize that we are beggars for whom someone has given attention. No wonder God considers the giving of thanks as a sacrifice to Him (Psalm 50:14). The giving of thanks is a way to magnify God (Psalm 69:30).

Prayers for All People (2:2-7)

Notice that these prayers are not to be made on the behalf of ourselves but for "everyone." If God kept a log of all of our prayers, and He put in one column the prayers we made on behalf of ourselves and put in another column the prayers we made on behalf of others, I wonder how the columns would look to us.

The one word that is repeated more than any other word in these few verses is the word *all*.

Verse 1: "Everyone"—literally, the Greek says "*all* men."

Verse 2: "*All* those in authority."

Verse 4: "*All* men."

Verse 6: "*All* men."

Why did Paul insist on including the word *all* so often? It was because of what was going on in the church at Ephesus. The Judaizers who wanted to be "teachers of the law" were teaching in such a way that excluded broad categories of people. Their system was exclusive; Christianity is inclusive. Those for whom we will not pray are those for whom we are not really open to evangelize or fellowship with.

It is difficult to pray for someone with whom you do not agree. It is also difficult to pray for someone who is in authority over you. Most people do not appreciate a chain of command if they are one of the bottom links in the chain. It would have been tough for the orthodox Jews to pray for the Roman kings and "all those in authority," for those were the people who were doing many things against Judaism. It would have been even tougher for Christians in that day to pray for the Roman leaders, for at this particular time in history, the Romans were antagonistic toward Christians. But rather than blame them, criticize them, or rebel against them, Paul wrote that they should pray for them.

To put that in modern terminology, Democrats are to pray for all decisions that a Republican President and Congress makes and vice versa. Political fences are to be crossed by prayer on behalf of others.

What a thing for the apostle Paul to write after having endured a Roman imprisonment. But there were several things that Paul knew that were relevant about praying for those in authority who may not agree with you:

1. People in kings' households can be saved (Philippians 1:12, 13; 4:21, 22).
2. By experiencing a Roman imprisonment, he knew the problems and punishments that many people were incurring who had been rebellious, either passively or actively, against authority.
3. Praying for *all* was one demonstration of "love, which comes from a pure heart and a good conscience and a sincere faith" (1 Timothy 1:5).
4. Praying for *all* squares with God and Jesus' concern for all. We then begin to apply 2 Corinthians 5:16, "So from now on we regard no one from a worldly point of view."

Without a break in the sentence, Paul gave a purpose for praying for all—"that we may live peaceful and quiet lives in all godliness and holiness."

To say "quiet lives" is an intensification of saying "peaceful lives." The Greek word translated "quiet" has little to do with our speech, but everything to do with our attitudes. This is the same word that is used in verse 12, where it is translated "silent." That fact will be very important when we study that portion of Scripture later.

Praying for those in authority will help us to lead a calm life in two ways. First, it will soften our attitudes toward them. Many times we are like Mount St. Helens, ready to explode when things don't go our way. But praying for others can give us inner quietness. We are not to be in perpetual turmoil because of those over us. Second, praying for others is one way that God uses to soften their attitudes toward us and to lessen their opposition against Christianity.

But praying for those in authority is not just so we can live in calmness, but also so that we can have lives that will be lived in "all godliness." That refers to reverence for God. Some translators translate the word "reverence," "piety," "respectful," "deeply religious," and "full observance of religion."

It is somewhat unfortunate that the NIV translators chose the word *holiness*. The Greek word does not express holiness, but rather dignity, high standards of morality, good moral character, and gravity in life-style. This word (or a derivative) is translated "noble" (Philippians 4:8) and "respect" (1 Timothy 3:4, 8, 11; Titus 2:2).

Paul was saying that we need to pray for our political leaders so that the country can have continual respect for God and high moral character as part of the fiber of that country. More than twenty great civilizations have risen and fallen in the history of the world. And all of them fell from inner decay. Is it possible that some fell because Christians neglected to pray for the authorities in those civilizations? God promised that if people would pray and repent, that God would heal the decaying disease in a country (2 Chronicles 7:14).

At the present time, some of the western culture—including the United States—is seeing a disintegration of respect for God, piety, commitment to the place of the church in culture, and a disintegration of moral character. Just observe what the mass media is doing. It would not have done that forty years ago. The first time a four-letter word was uttered in a movie, the nation was shocked. Today, every kind of perverted word imaginable is allowed to be heard in the movie theaters and is now invading the homes via television. Pornography is open; abortion is legal.

Christians need immediately to commit themselves to intercessory prayer for the leaders of our nation in order to stop the inner decay. We can no longer just blame the pagans. Christians must not be lazy in their spiritual responsibility to pray intercessory prayers. Yet this is seldom mentioned in our churches and is probably seldom expressed in the prayer times in our homes. If the church lets the government go without intercessory prayer, then why shouldn't God?

In the face of tough outer circumstances caused by the decisions of people over us, one way that demonstrates that we maintain our trust in God and that we do not react by just self-will is to pray in such a way that our thunder quiets down and our rampage gets calm.

The emphasis that we are to pray for all people is affirmed by the following:
1. It squares with God's approval: "This is good, and pleases God our Savior" (1 Timothy 2:3).
2. It meets with God's desire: "who wants all men to be saved and to come to a knowledge of the truth" (1 Timothy 2:4).
3. It squares with God's make-up: "For there is one God and one mediator between God and men, the man Christ Jesus" (1 Timothy 2:5).
4. It affirms God's actions: "who gave himself as a ransom for all men" (1 Timothy 2:6)
5. It is undergirded by the function of apostles: "And for this purpose I was appointed a herald and an apostle—I am telling the truth, I am not lying—and a teacher of the true faith to the Gentiles" (1 Timothy 2:7).

The whole point is that God is not exclusive, Jesus was not exclusive, and the apostles were not exclusive—so neither should we be in our prayers. God is not just wanting to be "our" Savior, but "their" Savior as well. He is one God. There is not one God for the whites and another for the blacks. There is not one God for the Jews and another for the Gentiles. There is not one God for the Americans and another for Russians. There is only *one* God, and He is for *all*—for all have come from one blood. God is not divided within himself, and He does not want mankind to be divided. Romans 10:12 captures it: "For there is no difference between Jew and Gentile—the same Lord is Lord of all and richly blesses all who call on him."

Since there is only one God, there is only one mediator between God and man. That mediator is Christ Jesus. All other religions that have their "saviors" are deceived. There is no one else who can bring us to God except Jesus. He said, "I am the way and the truth and the life. No one comes to the Father except through me" (John 14:6). On the positive side, He was saying that *everyone* can come to the Father through Him. That is true because He gave himself as a ransom for *all* men. With Jesus, there was—and is— no favoritism. The church that manifests favoritism in its practice and prayers is not carrying out the desires of Christ.

It is time for the hearts of churches to become bigger than their heads. In every community, there are people who are shut out from the church; there are those who will not enter the church building because they feel they are not welcome. It is time for the church to repent. We can open up to other people by praying for them, privately and publicly. That can change us inwardly.

Praying for *all* also applies to praying for Christians who are members of other congregations and denominations. Christians and churches must be more dedicated to live out Jesus' prayer for unity (John 17) than our history has shown. It is possible for our teachings and attitudes to build awfully tall walls—so tall that our students can never mature enough to see over them. As evangelical churches *can* we, *dare* we, *will* we develop disciples of Jesus who will help the whole family of God affirm our unity amidst our diversity?

As long as we are humans and can use our minds, we will have different understandings, opinions, and conclusions about various Bible teachings. Let our attitude be as follows: "In essentials unity, in nonessentials liberty, and in all things love." We cannot eliminate the diversity among us, but we must not tolerate the disunity, animosities, and alienations that so often accompany our differences.

God accepts our differences as we accept differences among the children in our families. But God rejects the arrogance that sometimes accompanies our differences. Hovering above all of our pet doctrines, hobby horses, and credal statements exists the one and only creed that makes an eternal difference. That creed is Christ. In Christ—and only in Christ—are we one. And we are one in Christ as Calvinists, as Arminians, as pre-millennialists, as post-millennialists, as a-millennialists, and as those who can't even spell the word or know what the word means.

Our unity is never rooted in conformity. If it is rooted in conformity, then none of us can have unity with anyone, including God. Our unity is always in Christ. There are no divisions among

Christians, either in the grave or in that world beyond the grave—there our divisions will come to an end. There Christians will affirm their unity. Shouldn't we pray that we can find it in our hearts to put an end to our short-lived divisions? If we would, we could leave a tremendous blessing behind us. Differences, yes. Various groupings around those differences, yes. But the failure to see brothers and the failure to treat them as brothers across the differences—no!

Recognizing the differences among us, yes. Talking about those differences, yes. But it is one thing to speak the truth (as we understand it) in love for the edification of our brother, and something else to speak to attack each other in order to prove another person wrong.

The Heavenly Father has made it clear that we are being *fitted together* and being *built together*. Let us not step out of God's fitting room or tear down what God is building.

What kind of communication would we give to the community and what kind of honor would we give to God if in our morning worship services, our prayers would include the other churches in our communities? Couldn't we ask God to bless the other worship services? Couldn't we ask God in our public worship to meet their needs? To pray for *all* men indeed means *all*.

Prayers in All Places and From All Postures (2:8)

A Place for Prayer

Many commentators suggest that the entirety of 1 Timothy 2 is outlining what should be going on in public worship. But there is not one hint in this chapter that the prayers mentioned, that the lifting up of holy hands, or that the activities of the women (verses 9-15) were restricted to worship services.

The only hint of the *place* is in verse 8: "everywhere." Other translations say, "in every place." Moffat says, "At any meeting of the church," but that is too restrictive. Paul was talking about life-style and expected spiritual responsibility in *every* place—not just in the assembly of worship.

A Posture for Prayer

Paul started verse 8 by saying, "I want." It is interesting to see what Paul wanted elsewhere. He used that Greek word five other times in his writings:

1. Philippians 1:12—he wanted the Philippians to know that his circumstances had worked for the furtherance of the gospel, and thus had been a benefit to others.
2. 1 Timothy 5:14—he wanted younger widows to marry for their own good and for the good of others.
3. Titus 3:8—he wanted Titus to speak confidently for the benefit of others.
4. 2 Corinthians 1:15—he wanted to come to the church for the kingdom's good.
5. Philemon 13—he wanted to keep Onesimus for the gospel.

It is interesting that all of Paul's stated wants were for the benefit of others. How do our wants stack up to that? Are our wants in more self-centered areas: I want a promotion; I want more pay; I want retirement benefits; I want a stereo; I want a car; I want a bigger house; I want security; I want to be loved?

No wonder Paul had an effective prayer life. His wants were unselfish. Is it possible that our prayer lives may not be as effective because our wants are turned inwardly too much? James made it clear, "When you ask, you do not receive, because you ask with wrong motives, that you may spend what you get on your own pleasures" (James 4:3).

When Paul said, "Lift up holy hands in prayer," he was spotlighting one posture for prayer. There is nothing that demands that we use that posture, but there is certainly nothing that suggests we should not.

There are several postures for prayer mentioned in the Bible. Below are some of them:
1. *Standing*. This suggests respect. There was a time in this country when younger people would stand when older people entered the room. That was a communication of respect.
2. *Heads bowed*. That communicates a spirit of humility and submission. That is still done when two people meet one another in some other cultures.
3. *Lifting the eyes upward*. That communicates that we expect our help to come from a source outside of us—God.
4. *Kneeling*. That communicates worship, adoration, and humility.
5. *Lying prostrate*. That suggests awe in the presence of God.
6. *Striking the breast*. That suggests a feeling of worthlessness in comparison to God's worthiness.

49

No posture of prayer is superior to any other. Nor should we discourage a person from a certain posture of prayer. Some people kneel often in prayer. Some people raise their hands. Some postures are connected to certain denominations, but that should not stop us from assuming any certain posture.

God hears our prayers regardless of our posture. We can pray as we drive our cars and be heard, but we would not want to bow our heads and close our eyes in this instance. We would not want to lift up both hands or lie prostrate.

The posture of prayer is really a non-verbal means of communication. It is body language with God. Posture should communicate what is going on inside of us. It is a communication from the inside out. We express outwardly something of what we are thinking inwardly.

Sometimes the external posture can affect our inwardness. That is because we are wholistically made. That happens in the normal process of living. For instance, there are times when you may wake up and feel in the pits. But you may say to yourself, "I'm not going to let this feeling determine my attitude today." You will purposely put on a smile and treat others cheerfully. And before long, you are feeling better. Your outward actions begin to change how you feel on the inside.

The non-verbal types of communication are important in effective communication. We are being told that only 7% of what makes communication effective comes from content; 38% comes from tone of voice; 55% comes from non-verbal signals. Wink at your wife, and you have said tons—but non-verbally. Hug her and whisper into her ear that you love her, and the non-verbal communication makes the verbal more effective.

Our posture should be a means of communication to God; however, our posture of prayer is not for a way of showing off so someone will conclude that we are super-spiritual. Neither is it to further our traditionalism—thinking that we must take this posture simply because that was how we were trained to pray.

What is the significance of the posture of lifting up hands? This posture is mentioned several times in the Bible. A study of those instances reveals to us many significant ideas.

It was a gesture of integrity. It was used for making a promise (Revelation 10:5). We still do that in human-to-human communication. If a person is taking an oath in a courtroom, he will be asked to raise his hand. If a person makes a commitment to go into the military service, he is asked to raise his hand. It is a symbol of making a promise. There are times when a person may want to pray with his hands uplifted because inside he is praying to God with a promise of a giving himself to the Father. He is communicating, "I am coming to you, God, with integrity."

It was a gesture of blessing. (See Luke 24:50; Leviticus 9:22; Psalm 134:2.) The raising of the hands for blessing is still used in many cultures. Indeed, God blesses us, but God is also to be blessed *by* us. We are to be involved in blessing the Lord. We may come to God in prayer with the attitude, "I want to bless you, Father, by my conversation with you at this time." A person with that kind of inner thinking may want to lift his hands to communicate that.

It was a gesture of friendship. A person can raise his hands to another to let him know that he is not coming in anger (2 Timothy 2:8) or as an enemy. The people in the first century were occupied by military forces and were divided in many different ways; so it was difficult to tell exactly who your enemy was. Everyone looked alike externally. So as one person approached another, he would often raise his hands to let that other person know that he came in peace and had no hidden weapons. He would be saying, "I am not coming to do battle; I am coming as a friend." Our gesture of reaching out to shake hands with someone goes back to this kind of communication—"I put my hand out to let you know it is empty and to receive you as a friend." Reaching out to hug another communicates this also.

There are times when things do not go our way. We can be discouraged and depressed. So we go to the Lord in prayer, but we do not want to go to Him to blame Him or to express anger. We can lift up our hands to communicate—"I am coming to you as a friend; I am not mad; I am not ticked off at you; I come to you with love." That can be a fantastic way to communicate our friendly approach if we really think and feel that on the inside.

It was a gesture of helping people who are neglected. (See Psalm 10:12.) It was used as a symbol of not forgetting or neglecting a person, in fact, of helping that person. God was asked to lift His hand to avenge the ones who were being mistreated, and when we lift up our hands to God, we are asking Him to take our hands and to use them in the same way God himself raises His hands to help. It is a prayer of intercession, but it is more than offering words in behalf of the people in need. It is a non-verbal communication to God that we are offering ourselves. It says, "Take my hands, Lord. Take me and use me to help this person or these people."

It was a gesture of need. (See Psalms 28:2, 88:9; Lamentations 2:19.) In that day, people who were beggars would raise their hands as they asked for alms. Beggars all across the world still do the same. To lift up our hands in prayer is to communicate to God our need for His help. It is to say, "I am empty-handed. I come to you as a beggar. All that I need must come from You. I need what You have to give." What a humble way of communication.

It was a gesture of longing for another. (See Psalms 63:1-4; 143:6.) This is still done today on a person-to-person basis. A child will lift up his hands in a gesture of longing for his parents. He wants to be picked up, embraced, and held. Lovers will reach out their hands to embrace. To lift up our hands in prayer can be a way of communicating to God that we yearn to touch Him, to be embraced by Him, to be hugged by Him. And it would not be inappropriate for the church, His Bride, to reach out in this way.

It was a gesture that communicated priority. (See Job 11:13.) It expressed the truth that the heart was directed upward.

It was a gesture of open acceptance. (See Isaiah 49:22; Proverbs 1:24.) It was a gesture of invitation and acceptance of other people. Even today, when you walk into an area and someone extends his hands to you, he is communicating acceptance and invitation. When we pray in this posture, we are telling God that we invite Him into our presence and that we accept Him.

It was a gesture of surrender. Although there is no clear reference of that in the Scriptures, it is used around the world to denote surrender. Lifting up of hands says, "I give up. I surrender; I am yours."

The lifting up of hands during prayer can be a marvelous way of non-verbally communicating to God, providing we are thinking some of the things the lifting up of hands is communicating. However, this posture should never be done as a pretentious show or to draw attention to oneself. Some people are offended when others around them lift their hands in prayer. But why would people be offended by the lifting up of hands? Have they made prejudgments because of traditionalism?

To lift up "holy" hands is to lift up hands set apart and dedicated to God for His use. It is not just the hands, but the whole person. Hands are for doing, for productivity. It would be like saying, "I am lifting up a life that is dedicated to God."

Summary Remarks About Prayer

What is the purpose of prayer? Some suggest that it is only to change us. They suggest that prayer does not change God. Prayer can change us, but it can also change God's mind.

Prayer can change us because of the philosophy of language. Our words are connected to our total being—mind, emotion, spirit, and body. That is the reason our words can affect our health (Proverbs 12:18). Words affect us because of two truths: the truth of our wholistic make-up and the truth of reinforcement. We hear the words we speak; when we hear them, they reenter our minds and reinforce inside of us what we have said.

Prayer can also change God's plans. Just look at some of the following passages: Exodus 32:9-14; 33:3, 15-17; 2 Samuel 24:16; 1 Kings 21:27-29; 2 Kings 20:1-6; Jeremiah 18:8; 26:19; 42:10; Joel 2:13, 14; Amos 7:1-6; Jonah 3:4-10.

God takes our prayers seriously. We are not just religiously play-acting or going through a ritual when we pray. Prayer makes a difference.

John Wesley once said, "God will do nothing on earth except in answer to believing prayer." That statement cannot be supported Biblically, but it may not be easily negated. It is true that God has given the responsibility of this planet to mankind. He may not invade this planet as readily as we think without being invited to do so. We should live our lives as if Wesley's statement were true.

Jesus emphasized that we invite God to be a part of our lives when He taught us to pray, "Your kingdom come, your will be done on earth as it is in heaven" (Matthew 6:10). We are inviting God's ruling might to overrule whatever is happening here. Prayer may be more the determining factor of what happens on earth than we have believed, lived, or taught.

But many people do not like this idea. Some would rather it depended on *their* activity, *their* study, *their* intellect, and *their* strategy. If prayer is really that needed and that important, then *they* are not in control. Prayer does challenge the ego.

Both prayer and practice are necessary. *Prayer* recognizes that the universe belongs to God. He is not enslaved by the laws of nature that He created. *Practice* recognizes that God has put man in a managerial role on this earth. The current disorder of things is more man's doing than we would like to admit.

Is it possible that we have become lazy with our spiritual responsibilities? Let us pray as if all depends upon God, and let's work as if it all depends upon us. He has *positioned* us as His ambassadors (2 Corinthians 5:17-19), and He has *empowered* us (2 Timothy 1:7; Ephesians 1:19; 3:17-19). We are to labor and strive "according to His power which mightily works within" us (Colossians 1:29, NASB).

We are both positioned and empowered. Let's tap the power with prayer, and let's tackle the position with practice.

CHAPTER FIVE

Christian Women

1 Timothy 2:9-15

Introduction

Women: Where do they belong in God's creation? What is their place in the church?

The male/female rift has been one of the most difficult to overcome through the ages. It may well be the last barrier that stands between human beings—a barrier that prevents us from loving *all* as Christ loves.

One of the first practical results of being a new person in Christ is to look at other people from a different perspective from the cultural perspective. We are to view others through God's eyes. This is one of the ways that we move out of living for ourselves and move to living for God (2 Corinthians 5:15-17).

It is difficult to see people properly when we have grown up looking at people through the glasses we have inherited from our culture. If our culture has taught us that a certain group of people is inferior, it is not easy to lay those glasses aside to see those people properly. And the longer we wear them, the more difficult it is to see clearly.

However, putting aside the old erroneous glasses is possible for us because we are new creatures in Christ. As new creatures, we ought to take on the ministry of reconciliation (2 Corinthians 5:18). To reconcile others to Christ, we must see them properly— which includes seeing women properly.

An Improper Look

It was difficult in the first century for people to look at women properly. Women had been belittled for hundreds of years. Greek philosophers taught that women were not fully human. It was believed that they were just one notch above the animal world and were to be treated more like property than persons.

In the eighth century before Christ, Hesiod taught that women were the embodiment of evil. In the fifth century before Christ, Herodotus taught that women were subordinated and were to be exploited. In the fourth century before Christ, Euripides taught that slaves and women were in the same category. During the second century before Christ, Semonides called women "swine."

Plato taught that the only reason women should be educated was to be able to get more out of them for the state. He also advocated that women should fight in wars. He taught that the punishment for men who were cowards and unrighteous was that they would be changed into women in their next life. He said that women are by nature secretive, undisciplined, and weak. He even taught that mothers were a threat to the character of their children because they were women.

Aristotle, who was a student of Plato and had great impact upon the thinking of the world at the time of Christ, taught that a woman was to a man what a slave was to a master. He said that a woman was an "unfinished" man, left standing on a lower step in the scale of development. He taught that males were superior to the females, that the man was to rule, and the woman was to be ruled.

The Greek philosophical teaching about women spread throughout the world because of the conquests of Alexander the Great, who was a student of Aristotle. This put-down of women began to filter into the Jewish mind. Jewish men praised and thanked God everyday that He did not make them Gentiles, slaves, or women—in that descending order. There is much thinking in Christianity today that is more of a carry-over of the pagan Greek view of women than a reflection of God's view.

God's View of Women

God created both men and women in His image (Genesis 1:27; 5:1, 2). God did not say that His creation was *very* good until after a woman joined the man. God consistently used women as well as men in effective roles in His kingdom. (For a comprehensive study of this, see Julia Staton's book, *What the Bible Says About Women,* College Press, Joplin, MO.)

There were times when God used women to save the whole nation of Israel (midwives saved Jewish boys from Pharaoh of Egypt, and Queen Esther intervened to save the entire Jewish nation). God used a woman to judge and lead the nation for a time—Deborah (Judges 4). A judge in that day was the religious, civil, and military leader of the entire nation. Women were also prophets of the Lord—those persons inspired by God to speak on His behalf. (See Exodus 15:20; Judges 4:4; 2 Kings 22:14; 2 Chronicles 34:22, Isaiah 8:3; Luke 2:36; Acts 21:9.)

Women wrote hymns, were chosen by God to be queens, prayed, spoke for God, ruled the nation, brought sacrifices, took the Nazirite vow, served at the entrance of the tabernacle, and led in worship. Some women were wiser than their husbands and made decisions that reversed their husbands' wishes (Abigail). Some owned and ran businesses, purchased real estate, and managed large households with several employees.

However, even in light of all of the above instances, which God blessed, Jewish women still considered marriage and giving birth to children their most cherished role. They considered this role to be their greatest contribution.

Jesus maintained a high respect for womanhood, as did God. He condemned men who lusted after women (Matthew 5:28). He called a halt to men's divorcing their wives for liberal reasons (Matthew 5:31, 32; 19:1-9). He told parables in which women had key roles (Matthew 13:33; Luke 15:8-10); He fed hungry women as well as hungry men (Matthew 14:21). He commended the faith of women as well as that of men (Matthew 15:28); He commended women for ministering to Him (Matthew 26:10). He even commanded that wherever the gospel was preached, the service of one woman should be included (Matthew 26:13). He cast out unclean spirits out of women as well as men (Mark 7:25-30). He raised a girl from the dead (Mark 5:35-43).

Two of Jesus' closest friends were women (John 11:5). Jesus allowed women to follow Him from place to place and financially support Him (Luke 8:1-3). He allowed a woman to tell others, including men, about Him (John 4). He allowed a woman to anoint Him for burial (Matthew 26:12). One of His favorite places to visit was the house of a woman (Luke 10:38; John 12:1, 2). Jesus taught Martha that a woman needs more fulfillment than just being a worker in the kitchen (Luke 10:40-42). Jesus commissioned women to tell His disciples that He had risen—thus they were the first proclaimers of the resurrection (Matthew 28:1-11; Mark 16:1-7; John 20:1, 2).

It is quite clear that one of the marks of the Christian age is that God would enable both men and women to prophesy—

proclaim—His message. He would pour out His Spirit on both men and women, which would result in both men and women's carrying out the charisma and power of God's Spirit (Acts 2:17, 18).

It is apparent that women did indeed both pray and proclaim in the public assembly (1 Corinthians 11:3-16). The issue in that section of Scripture is not that the women were doing wrong by praying or prophesying, but in the way they were presenting themselves physically in public.

Women in the Silent Chamber

If a person had an assignment of reading the Bible from Genesis to Revelation to discover whether or not God had put women in the silent chamber of life (that is, she was not to speak about God in public and particularly not to men), he would not find such a treatment of women until 1 Corinthians 14:34, 35. It seems clear to me that Paul was not referring to females in general in that text, but to wives in particular who were disrupting a worship service by asking their husbands questions audibly. The word *women* in verse 34 should be translated "wives" as the word *men* in verse 35 is translated "husbands."

Three chapters earlier (1 Corinthians 11), Paul spoke about women who were praying and prophesying and did not give any hint that it was improper. The issue in 1 Corinthians 14 is the disruption of the worship service due to the inappropriateness of asking questions out loud to husbands who were seated in a different location, as was the custom.

The only other text that might put a woman in the silent chamber is the passage under consideration—1 Timothy 2:9-15. Although this text has been used to prevent women from speaking in a worship service, that usage has several problems attached to it:
1. Such an understanding does not fit the wholistic study of what the Bible says about women and how they have served God through the ages.
2. Such an understanding assumes that this is referring to a woman's place in the church assembly only. However, there is not one word in this chapter that refers to the church assembly. The only location that is referred to in this chapter is the word *everywhere* in verse 8.
3. Such an understanding fails to translate the Greek word as "wives" and applies the verses to all women.

A Wife's Relationship to Her Husband

That this section of Scripture was referring to a wife's relationship with her husband and was not putting a woman (because she is female) into a silent chamber is clear for the following reasons:

(1) There is no separate Greek word for the word *wife;* it is the same as the word *woman.* The same Greek word *(gyne)* refers to both. In order to tell which is being referred to, we need to study the context carefully. In some places, it clearly means a woman, as her gender identification. In other places, it refers to a wife, such as in Matthew 1:20; Acts 5:1; Ephesians 5:22; Colossians 3:18; 1 Timothy 3:2; 1 Peter 3:1; and at least seventy-five other places in the New Testament.

(2) Anytime the apostle Paul used the words *woman* and *man* together and talked about submission, he was always referring to a wife's relationship to her husband. And that is what he did here.

(3) What Paul said about a woman in this passage is nearly identical (using some of the very same concepts) to what Peter said in 1 Peter 3:1-6. There is no good, objective reason to say that Peter was talking about husband/wife relationships while Paul was not.

(4) Paul said, "I do not permit a woman to teach or to have authority over a man; she must be silent" (1 Timothy 2:12). But that did not square with Paul's own practice—*if* it meant that a female had to be silent in the presence of a male. Paul did permit women to pray and prophesy in the assembly (1 Corinthians 11). Paul did not suggest that women did not receive any of the gifts of the Spirit that he mentioned in 1 Corinthians 12. Paul did not prevent Philip's four daughters from prophesying (Acts 21:9). Paul did not criticize Priscilla for team teaching with her husband Aquilla (Acts 18:24-26).

(5) Adam and Eve (the example given) were the first male and female, but they were also the first husband and wife.

(6) When Paul mentioned "childbearing" (1 Timothy 2:15), he was surely not suggesting that every female, regardless of her marital status, should become a mother. He was referring to wives' being fulfilled in bringing up children, not in trying to rule their husbands.

(7) The words *quietness* and *silent* do not at all refer to not speaking audibly. Those words were used to describe a gentle, tranquil spirit. The word *silent* in verse 12 is exactly the same Greek word translated "quiet" in verse 2. If the word *silent* meant

not being allowed to speak out loud, then Paul was asking men to pray for the authorities so that no one could open his mouth and speak. Notice the word's usage in 2 Thessalonians 3:12; 1 Timothy 2:2; and 1 Peter 3:4—they refer to a gentle, quiet spirit. A good translation of the word would be "calm."

(8) The kind of teaching that the wife was not permitted to do was the authoritative kind that made her master over her husband (1 Timothy 2:12).

The Greek word *(authenteo)* is not used any other place in the New Testament, nor was it used in the Greek translation of the Old Testament. It was the strongest word in the Greek language to describe someone who was functioning as an independent, domineering, mastering autocrat. The Greek word literally means "to set apart self from someone else." It was such a strong word for picturing a person's total independence from someone else that it was used in the second century to describe murder. It was used to describe someone who had the attitude that he did not need the other person.

To suggest that a wife has nothing at all to teach her husband is extremely misleading and certainly not realistic. At the very outset, God created the woman as a helper fit or suitable for her husband. There would be no "help" without some teaching.

However, that kind of teaching should not slip into a domineering attitude of independence from the husband. Paul made it very clear that in the Lord, a woman—wife—is not independent of a man—husband—nor is the man—husband—independent of the woman—wife (1 Corinthians 11:11).

A Wife's Transparency (2:9, 10)

In these verses, Paul was describing a wife's relationship to her husband, demanding that it go beyond superficiality. A relationship that is lasting is based upon what is on the inside, not what is on the outside. It is so easy to get caught up in the competitive world that evaluates persons according to what they see in the mirror. So Paul stressed that the wife's relationship to her husband should be based upon character, not coverings. On the inwardness, not the outwardness. Upon what is at first invisible, not what is first visible. What cannot be purchased, not what can be purchased and put on the body. What wears well, not what wears out. What is spiritual, not what is physical.

No one can really know what a person is by what that person wears. A person is known by what he/she does. A person's real self comes from the inside out, not from the outside in. A husband/wife relationship that is lasting is based upon what is eternal, not what is temporary.

Paul was certainly not suggesting that a wife should not care how she looks to her husband. He was, instead, correcting an over-emphasis that many women had succumbed to in the first century and still continue to do today.

Some wives can spend so much time in front of the mirror that they become more concerned about how they look to others than about how they treat others. A wife can look great but be a grouch. She can look sensational, but be insensitive to her husband. He can be proud of her in public, but dread to spend time alone with her.

The main issue in the woman's looks is modesty. Paul was not suggesting that a woman should not be concerned about the looks of her hair, or that she cannot wear jewelry, or that she cannot wear expensive clothes. However, she should not be known primarily for those things. What she is on the inside should match how she looks on the outside.

In summary, Paul was stressing that a wife's greatest asset is what she is in her heart, not what she has in her closet. Some women are known first of all because of their jewelry, hairstyles, clothing, automobiles, and other glamorous items. Paul meant that real meaningfulness comes by being known most of all for one's "good deeds." Those are deeds that benefit others and that should be expressed in the wife/husband relationship. Those are deeds that demonstrate that she worships God rather than gadgets. They show that she has priorities in what is eternal and lasting, not what is temporary. Faith outlives fads. Her focus is primarily on others and upon God.

The wife who prioritizes what she wears and how she looks has her focus primarily upon herself. That can seriously weaken the marriage relationship.

The Wife as a Humble Learner/Teacher (2:11, 12)

For Paul to say that "a woman should learn" was a revolutionary idea for much of the first-century culture. Women were often prevented from learning. Some rabbis taught that it was a waste of time to teach the Torah to women. Over against that restriction, Paul wrote that a woman *should* learn. A woman's capacity is not less than a man's. A woman has as much right to learn as a man. Having been denied something for so long, it would be easy for attitudes to become embittered and for women to start demanding their rights. Consequently, Paul discussed the attitude a woman should manifest in her learning. Those attitudes are described by the words *quietness* and *full submission*. They stress peace, tranquility, humility, and mutual respect.

That a woman has nothing to teach a man (1 Timothy 2:12) does not square with the rest of the Scriptures. Therefore, this text was probably discussing the wife's attitude in teaching her husband. (See the discussion above.) Every husband knows the significance of the two-way sharing between a husband and wife. A wife cannot be a true "help" if her husband is not open for her to do any teaching at all (Genesis 2:18). This text prohibits a wife from teaching with an independent and arrogant attitude. (See the discussion on the word *authority*.) The truth is that no one should teach others with those kinds of attitudes. But having been put down for so many years, women were evidently developing the wrong kind of attitudes, which were damaging marriage relationships.

The "silent" wife (1 Timothy 1:12) is one who is tranquil, peaceful, and delightful to be around. *Full submission* refers to having full respect for the husband, which is translated into serving his needs. Submission is not the exclusive role of the woman. No one was more submissive than Jesus. It is a mark of humility and love. It sees a need and reaches out to meet that need in selfless service.

Submission begins with an attitude that is transferred into actions. The attitude is that of Christlikeness; Christ did not consider equality with God something to be grasped, but emptied himself of "ego" so He could fill himself with the attitude and activities of a servant. While some like to dump the concept of submission onto the woman only, it is to be a characteristic of each member of the church. It is to be one aspect of how we treat each other.

Prior to writing about wives' submitting to their husbands, Paul wrote about church members' submitting to one another: "Submit to one another out of reverence for Christ" (Ephesians 5:21). Submission within the family of God is to begin and be modeled within the family at home.

When Paul wrote that we are to submit to one another, he summed up all that he had been saying about proper relationships within the church, beginning with Ephesians 4. There he dealt practically with how to maintain unity amidst diversity. The specific ways include humility, gentleness, patience, bearing one another's burdens, using gifts for one another, not staying angry, using the tongue to build up one another, getting rid of negative interpersonal relationships (such as bitterness, slander, and malice), being kind and compassionate, forgiving each other, living a life of love, and not being immoral (Ephesians 4:1—5:20). All of these attitudes and actions are summed up in the general statement, "Submit to one another."

Mutual submission is the opposite of mutual control. We can control people we do not like—in fact, we may despise them. But real submission happens because we value others. Thus, we voluntarily give up rights and demands for the good of others. Submission is the ability to give up the terrible burden of always needing to get our way. Submission is the freedom to give in to each other because we care about each other. It is an expression of unconditional love. It is not the attitude or activity of an inferior person. Jesus was certainly not inferior, and neither is any member of His body. And neither is the wife inferior to the husband.

When one understands that rabbinic teaching prohibited women from teaching small children, then we realize how easy it would be for bitterness to rage in the hearts of some of the women. Why learn if she is not permitted to teach? But in that teaching role, she should not do so with a war-like attitude.

The Need for Partnership (2:13, 14)

Partnership and interdependence are seen in the creation itself. Eve was not formed independently from Adam. Nor was Adam formed without Eve in mind. Husbands and wives need each other.

Some see these two verses as an order of creation showing man's superiority over the woman. The better approach is to note the interdependence of the mates. "For as woman came from man, so also man is born of woman. But everything comes from God" (1 Corinthians 11:12)

As women become liberated from many other restrictions that put them down, they should not feel that that frees them to be independent from their husbands. Both husbands and wives need to help each other to resist the onslaughts of Satan. Eve failed to do that in the Garden of Eden. The devil got her by herself and enticed her to make a decision totally independent from her husband. But it was a decision that both of them had discussed earlier.

She was "deceived"; she was not mean, deceptive, evil, or inferior. What happened to Eve has happened to all of us. She was deceived or tricked. That can happen more easily when we "go it alone." That happens when we get prideful and think we don't need others. That is a major reason that pride comes before a fall. The devil can do more against a person who is filled with pride than in any other single situation.

Some like to suggest that Adam was not deceived because he was superior to Eve. But there is no evidence that Paul meant that.

A Wife's Fulfillment (2:15)

Some texts say that women will be saved, others say "kept safe." However we express it, the issue is certainly not eternal salvation. Salvation comes only through belief in Jesus Christ (John 3:6-18; 14:6). Childbearing does not give a woman eternal salvation. It is a biological function, not a spiritual security blanket. Women can be saved who have never married. Wives can be saved who never have children.

Then what was Paul saying? The Greek word for *safe* or *saved* is a word that also means to be made whole. It was used to describe people who had been healed of diseases. That healing brought them to functional wholeness. In context, this verse was discussing the wife's relationship to her husband. She shall have wholeness in that relationship, not by trying to dominate him, but by rearing their children. Paul was emphasizing that women should be devoted to their children. No one else can really replace their motherhood role. But that does not mean that is the only thing women are to do.

Some have explained this expression in the following ways:
1. She will be kept physically safe through childbearing. Yet many women have died in that process.
2. She will be kept safe eternally. But childbearing is not a substitute for the cross of Jesus and acceptance of Him.
3. She will be kept safe through *the* Child bearing—referring to the birth of Jesus. That is really stretching the point. We are

not saved by Jesus' birth, but by His death and resurrection. And it is not only women who are saved by the coming of Christ.

4. She will be kept safe from a meaningless life in which she has to compete with a man for usefulness and uniqueness. This idea has merit.

5. She will be kept safe from seeking to live a totally independent life (1 Timothy 2:13, 14), and from an inappropriate relationship with her husband (1 Timothy 2:11, 12), and from an out-of-balance prioritizing attention given to herself (1 Timothy 2:9, 10). This seems to fit the context best.

Summary

Paul was dealing with the husband/wife relationship that was evidently getting out of balance in the church at Ephesus. Wives are to live in submission to their husbands, not as independent autocrats over them.

The problem with the first husband and wife (Adam and Eve) was that Eve began to act independently from her husband. When the devil got her to start thinking independently rather than as a partner with her husband, he was able to deceive her—which resulted in their downfall.

A wife will not become whole by trying to "bring up" her husband, but she will be fulfilled by "bringing up" her children. The words *kept safe* in the Greek describe completeness or wholeness that contributes to a person's sense of security on the inside.

Application for Us Today

Those who feel that Paul was teaching that a female cannot teach a male and that it is to be applied today need to be consistent in how it is carried out.

God expects us to apply Scripture to the level of understanding we have. If Paul was saying that a female cannot teach a male, he meant that a female could not teach any male (regardless of age) in any place or on any topic. In this text, no chronological age was mentioned, or the location of the teaching, or the topic the woman was teaching.

If it is wrong by the order of creation for a female to teach a male, then it would be wrong for her to teach any age male in any place on any topic. The Scripture does not support this interpretation. From Genesis 1 to 1 Timothy 2, God had not put His women into a silent chamber; and, in my judgment, did not do it in this section of Scripture either.

At the same time, this does not give women the right to force a teaching situation in the assembly if the cultural stance of that assembly is not ready to accept it. A mature Christian understands those rights, but with the fruit of the Spirit—which includes patience and gentleness—lives out his or her life without demanding those rights.

Women as well as men are important and functional members of the body of Christ and have God-given gifts. One is not superior to the other because of sexual gender. Let us recognize the mutual abilities we have, and let us also recognize the abilities and responsibilities that are different. Women should not try to act like men, and men should not treat women as if they were second-rate. We need each other. May we demonstrate unity amid our differences. Let us take off our cultural glasses, look at each other as God sees us, and break down the wall of separation between the sexes.

Is it possible that future historians may declare the irony of ironies—that in the middle of the twentieth century, business managers did more toward emancipating women than did the church? To say that these have done it for money removes none of the sting, for it is a humiliation that pagans searching for more money effect the good that Christians fail to effect for love. There is some evidence that the sexual segregation may make its last stand in the church.

CHAPTER SIX

Leaders for the Church

1 Timothy 3

A Noble Task (3:1)

From Status to Service

Some people had probably been eager for the position of overseer, while others were critical that some desired that responsibility. Paul said that anyone who aspires to be an overseer in the church should not be criticized, for what he is really desiring is not a title, not a status symbol, not a hierarchical office, but rather "a noble task." That means a work that is official. It is a good work, and a good work calls for a good worker.

Some translators use the word "*office* of overseer." Some see the word *office* emphasizing status. But it is an office of service, not of superiority. Many offices exist to serve people. When the service is not needed, there is no reason for the office. For instance, the office of a senator or congressman is to serve the people of his area. The same principle applies to the office of overseer; he who desires that office desires to be a servant.

Terms That Describe the Task

There are two Greek words that describe the overseer. Both words describe a person functioning as a servant to others. One term is *presbuteros,* which is often translated "elder." It is a term that describes anyone who is an older person. It is the same word used for "older man" in 1 Timothy 5:1. The other term is *episkopos,* which is translated as "bishop" or "overseer." These two terms are interchangeable in usage, as seen in such places as Acts 20:17-28 and Titus 1:5-9.

Why then are there two terms for the same function? *Elder* describes a person who is mature. It does not necessarily mean a person in this leadership role has to be old chronologically, but he does need to be "grown up" spiritually. *Overseer* describes the function or the kind of service this person renders.

To translate *episkopos* as "overseer" instantly gives us some problems, because many people have differing ideas of what an "overseer" does. Is he a military-type, such as a general or sergeant? Is he a warden-type? Is he a supervisor? Is he like a foreman? Is he an inspector? Is he to act like the chairman of a board of directors of a corporation might act? All of these highlight status and authority, but none of these capture the New Testament concept of what is meant for an "overseer" of the church.

It is important to consider how the verb for the term is used in the New Testament. While the noun *(episkopos)* spotlights the person, the verb *(episkeptomai)* emphasizes the activity of that person. By researching how the verb is used, we can conclude that an "overseer" is really someone who looks upon people for the purpose of looking after them. The verb describes serving people's needs.

Below are some places where this verb is used, although the English translation reads "visit," "care for," "be concerned about," or some other phrase:

1. Matthew 25:36, 43. This reference is to a physically sick person who needed an "overseer" to look after him.
2. Luke 7:16. Here the verb is translated "to help." It describes ministry.
3. Acts 7:23. "Visit" is the translation, and it describes Moses, who had come to his people for the purpose of relieving them of some of their physical burdens.
4. Hebrews 2:6. "Care for"; it is describing how God cares for those who could easily be overlooked and neglected.
5. James 1:27. Here the verb is translated "to look after." It talks about ministry to people in distress.

The greatest personal model of this type of activity is Jesus himself. In fact, He is referred to as our "Overseer" (1 Peter 2:25). He looked upon people for the purpose of looking after them. He did not "look over" them to communicate superiority. He emptied himself and became humble so He could serve man's needs (Philippians 2:5-11).

The most accurate professional or career model of what was meant by "overseer" is that of a shepherd. The images of overseer and shepherd are linked together in several places (i.e. Acts 20:28; 1 Peter 2:25; 5:1-4).

A shepherd spends time with his sheep, protects his sheep, talks with his sheep, knows his sheep, seeks for the lost and/or straying sheep, provides for the physical needs of his sheep, and rescues his sheep. All of this tells us that this function is indeed a "noble task." To emphasize its status and not its service is to misunderstand the function of an "overseer" in the church.

To summarize: these people are the leaders in the church who have a specific task of seeing to it that the various needs of the members (spiritual, social, physical, and material) are met. These men don't necessarily meet all those needs *personally.* But they do see that the structure and the resources are designed and available to meet those needs, as well as delegating responsibilities to those who have the expertise to serve in the various ways.

Overseers (3:2-7)

God is not looking for better methods, but for better men. God's method is people. The qualifications in this passage are not listed in order to tell us who the first-rate citizens of the kingdom are. They should be seen more as attitudinal characteristics; these are the attitudes (and aptitudes) that are needed to meet the various needs of the members of the body.

To meet the needs, these men would have to do some of the following: teaching, leading out as examples of righteousness, protecting, discipling, comforting, providing security, soothing the troubled, forgiving, handling disputes, evaluating weaknesses, selecting and delegating responsibilities, helping the grieving, reminding people of God's Word, counseling, ministering to the sick, and evangelizing—just to name a few.

What characteristics would be required to carry out these services effectively? They are listed here in this passage for us.

Marital Designation

Because of the time that is necessary to spend with people of both sexes, it is important for a man to be married and have a good relationship base at home with sexual satisfaction. Without this, the temptations would escalate.

"The husband of but one wife" is a difficult phrase to nail down with a precise meaning. The Greek literally reads, "a one-woman man." It is not possible to decide on the *exact* meaning of that phrase. It is important for each congregation to decide its own understanding and then make its decisions based on that.

Here are some possible meanings:

1. A man must be married at the time he serves.
2. If a person is married, he must be married only once.
3. A man whose wife has died is no longer qualified.
4. A man cannot have experienced a divorce any time in his life.

The big issue facing the church today is whether or not a man who has experienced a divorce can serve as an overseer. Again, each congregation must make that decision based on its understanding of this text.

Here are some ways that some churches apply this passage:

1. A man can serve as an elder if his divorce was prior to the time he became a Christian.
2. A man can serve as an elder if his divorce was on Scriptural grounds, and he was the "innocent party."
3. A man cannot serve as an overseer if there has been a divorce at any time for any reason.
4. A man can serve as an overseer if he is married to only one wife at the present time and has the other characteristics listed.

Whatever we do with this issue must be consistent with what we do with the rest of the characteristics. If we require that all of the other characteristics describe a man's total life-style throughout his entire past, then the issue of divorce should be treated the same way. But if we conclude that the characteristics are dealing with a man's spiritual maturity in his present stage of life, then we should deal with divorce in the same way. Would we disqualify a man whom we discovered was a lover of money twenty years ago, but now through God's strength has a generous spirit? If not, then we should consider allowing a man to be an overseer who has a good marriage now, although he may have experienced a divorce in his past. We may want to affirm that God can do tremendous things in a man's life even though there has been some negative history. Don't we all have skeletons in our closets?

Some suggest that using someone who has never been divorced, regardless of the timing or situation, would be a model for the community to emphasize the sacredness of marriage. And it certainly would.

Others suggest that using a man who has gone through a divorce but has grown into Christlikeness since then would be a model to the community that God is a God of forgiveness, of recycling people, and of reconciling people to himself and to His purpose on earth. That would also be true.

It is also possible for a person to be married for over fifty years to the same woman and not be a "one-woman man." He might be unfaithful. Or it might also be possible that he is sexually faithful but does not care for her, does not love her, does not provide for her, and/or does not communicate with her. Being a one-woman man really refers to being committed to one's wife. The man who has the ability and practice of being committed to his wife may be able to be committed to the bride of Christ—the church.

Personal Qualifications

1. Above reproach. It is possible that this qualification is an umbrella under which all of the others fall. To be above reproach certainly does not mean that the man has never made mistakes. Peter called himself a "fellow elder" (1 Peter 5:1), but at one time Jesus turned to Peter and said, "Get behind me, Satan! You are a stumbling block to me; you do not have in mind the things of God, but the things of men" (Matthew 16:23). We are all familiar with the way Peter turned his back upon Jesus and denied even knowing the Man from Nazareth.

The word literally means having nothing to take hold upon. It is spotlighting the fact that there is to be nothing in the man's present character, as seen in his conduct, that would discredit the moral commitment of God. Many suggest that there should be nothing in the man's character, belief, or conduct that would cause unsaved people to criticize the church. But I think that is going too far. To make that the criterion is to allow the secular world to write the agenda for the church. It would cause the leaders of the church to walk on eggshells so that people in the community would not disapprove of them.

However, it doesn't take long studying the life of Christ to see how many criticized Him. Many things Jesus said and did were thought to be immoral by people who evaluated morality and immorality by their own traditions. Elders, and thus the church, may be, and in many situations ought to be, criticized for the stance they take. But to be above reproach is to be able to show that the position and practice is consistent with Jesus' own position and practice. We must root our behavior in the grace and truth of Jesus, not in the expectations of people who may be professional nit-pickers.

The word *must* comes from a little Greek word *(dei)* that stresses the moral necessity of being above reproach. It is possible that many elders have not enjoyed the flexibility, the openness, and the joy of living out their Christianity because of the fear that somebody is going to criticize something they do. I remember that at one time it was considered to be wrong for an elder to be up front in a colored dress shirt instead of a white one. I remember when it was considered to be immoral for an elder to have a pool table in his home, to attend any kind of movie, to change the order of the worship service, to do any kind of work on Sunday. (Remember the criticisms Jesus got for doing good on the Sabbath?)

The many commentators who use this phrase to suggest that the church's leaders must conduct their lives in such a way that neither they or the church gets any criticism or receives any attack from the outsiders have done us a terrible injustice. If Jesus lived His life like that, He would not have been crucified.

To be above reproach is to live our lives so that they square with the moral character of our Lord himself. It is to allow the new divine nature, the Holy Spirit, to fill us rather than the human spirit. When the Holy Spirit moves in, my own spirit still remains. The two are at odds with one another (Romans 7). An elder must be a living demonstration of what it means to allow the Holy Spirit's nature to be expressed in all of his relationships—at work, at home, in business, in finances, in the public, and in private.

To be above reproach is to put on the new self, which is in the likeness of God (Ephesians 4:24). Good additional checkpoints would be the specifics in Ephesians 4:25—6:20.

2. Temperate. This word comes from a word that means wineless. It suggests that a man does not allow his mind to get clouded up, confused, or intoxicated with philosophies, principles, hobby horses, or tangents that detour from God's central principles. The same word is translated in 2 Timothy 4:5 as "keep your head." This refers to the person who keeps his head when others are losing theirs. He remains calm; he remains cool; he is slow to jump into the middle of a fire and add more fuel to it. This does not characterize a person only in the church, but in all of his relationships—in the community as well as in the church.

3. Self-controlled. To be self-controlled is consistent with being temperate. This describes the person who is well-behaved in actions and reactions. He can walk in a world filled with temptations because he keeps his body under control and makes his body his slave, rather than being a slave to his body (1 Corinthians

9:27). Here is the man who has made a covenant with his eyes not to look lustfully at women (Job 31:1). Here is the man who has resolved not to sin with his mouth (Psalm 17:3). Here is the man who lives by commitment, not just by feeling.

Living by commitment rather than by feeling was what Jesus modeled in the Garden of Gethsemane when He asked for that cup to be taken away from Him, but then prayed that not His will, but God's, be done. It is not always easy, but it is essential.

It happened a few years ago in Carmel-By-The-Sea in California. A couple of young lads were surfing when the wind caught one of them and blew him out to sea. He could not handle the situation and was drowning. A man walking by heard the screams. He dived into the water, swam to the boy, grabbed him, and pushed him to shore. The boy's life was saved, but the man drowned. For three or four days, he was dubbed "the mystery man" because he had no identification. Then he was identified.

He was twenty-nine years old—in the prime of life. He loved children dearly, but he feared water terribly. He was at a crossroads of decision when he heard the screams of that boy—between a commitment to the lives of children and a feeling of fear. Love and commitment overcame fear.

There will be many times when leaders of the church will stand at the crossroads of making a commitment that we know we should make, but at the same time fearing the reaction of the people, either in the church or in the community. Which will determine our decision?

The man who lives by commitment is not culturally-controlled, media-controlled, peer-controlled, fear-controlled, crowd-controlled, tradition-controlled, or criticism-controlled. Here is the man who is self-controlled because he is Spirit-controlled. He is not tossed by every wave that comes. He thinks straight. Such a person can save a committee meeting, can help motivate the church into new ministries and new methodologies, and can calm the storms because there is a calmness on the inside.

4. Respectable. This comes from the word from which we get our word *cosmetics*. It comes from the same root as the word for the orderly world. It denotes an inward orderliness seen in an outward adornment or beauty. It is the same word that is used in 1 Timothy 2:9 to describe how a woman should be dressed (modestly). Here it is describing a man's outward conduct of good behavior that comes from his inner character of Christlikeness.

73

While being temperate and self-controlled both stress his inwardness, to be respectable stresses his outwardness, so these three words together show a unity, an integration of what he is on the inside with what he appears to be on the outside. It shows that his character and reputation do not contradict each other.

To be respectable does not mean everyone agrees with you. But even though they disagree, they respect the basis for your position and behavior. They know that it comes out of sincerity.

While it is true that our English word *cosmetics* comes from this word, it is untrue that we should over-emphasize that point. There are two kinds of cosmetics. One kind is a cover-up; it covers up what is really there. The other kind is a revealer; it highlights and brings out what is already there. A person who is truly respectable is a person who highlights and brings out the character of Christ, who is already in the heart.

5. *Hospitable.* This literally means "a lover of strangers." This stresses a person who is not a respecter of persons. He is friendly, warm, and responsive to others. People feel at ease with him. An elder is to be a person who is a friend. Jesus was seen as the friend of sinners before they caught on that He was to be their Savior or Lord. A church filled with hospitable elders will be a church that is open to visitors, and those visitors will feel this church has a heart open to them. We are living in a very impersonal world today. As we move into a more high-tech society, where people will be working more with machines than with people, the church can have its most successful growth if the church truly becomes a people with open arms and hearts.

One mark of the church of Jesus is to be other-oriented. A church that does not attract outsiders is a church that is too indrawn. Such a church needs to look at the hospitable nature of her leaders. It is interesting that many of the kinds of people that flocked to Jesus are the same kinds of people today that feel so uncomfortable with the leaders of the church. To be hospitable is to be an ambassador of the friend-Jesus, not a communicator of past personal prejudices, narrowness, and exclusiveness.

The more a person is a dictator, the less he will be hospitable. John sharply criticized a man named Diotrephes who was not hospitable (3 John 9, 10). It is not enough to have correct heads filled with principles, if we have cold hearts with people.

6. *Able to teach.* To be able to teach is far more than just being a walking encyclopedia of doctrine. Teaching is a *charisma* from

God (Romans 12:7; Ephesians 4:11). We may one day discover that we have hindered the body of Christ by choosing elders without a consideration of their being gifted by God to teach. Part of the pastoring responsibilities of the elder comes through the activity of teaching.

Some have really copped out on this qualification by saying that this refers to the elder's *ability* to teach, but not that he should *actually* teach. One who is able to teach because he is gifted to teach has the moral responsibility to function with that gift in and for the church. Just being able to talk in front of people is not necessarily a proof of being gifted to teach. Who is really listening? Whose lives are being changed? Who is being excited? Who is being discipled into Christlikeness?

7. Not given to drunkenness. Literally, this refers to a person who is "not beside wine." He doesn't always have a filled wine-glass in his hand. He is not a continuous drinker (Titus 1:7). This is not a word that calls for total abstinence; however, in this culture with alcoholism so high, an elder should probably model total abstinence in order not to be a stumbling block to someone who is wrestling with the alcohol problem. Jewish people diluted their wine several times over with water to make sure it was not too strong. No commercial wine today follows that pattern. Because of the impurity of water, wine was used for an entirely different purpose than supporting the alcohol industry today. We must not permit the traditional use of diluted wine to give us the green light for the status symbol of drinking alcohol, which bombards us in this self-centered, pleasure-seeking society.

8. Not violent, but gentle. This describes the person who is not always looking for another fight. He doesn't always have his theological six-shooter drawn in order to shoot down someone else's position. When there are differences between himself and another, he is considerate of the other person (gentle). He is able to be kind and can correct people with the gentleness that can lead them into repentance and truth rather than dictating to them in roughness (2 Timothy 2:24, 25).

9. Not quarrelsome. The elder must be a peacemaker, not a peace breaker. This does not mean that he will never engage in controversy, but he knows how to disagree agreeably. He knows what it means to have differences without animosities. He knows how to have commitments without compromise, but at the same time not declaring combat. He knows the essentials upon which unity is to be based. He also knows the nonessentials in which liberty is to be allowed. He knows that in all things, love is to reign.

10. Not a lover of money. This does not mean that he is poor or mad at the rich. Anyone who is mad at the rich would be very uncomfortable with God, for no one is richer than He. But here is a person who is not greedy and reaching out for more for himself. He knows that there is a difference between owning property and possessions and being owned by them. An elder who is a lover of money at his job and with his family will eventually be a lover of money at the church, and his first response to any needed ministry will be, "How much will it cost?"

It is time that our leaders quit thinking about the cost factor as the determining criterion. They should think about how much the ministry is needed in the community and how much it would represent the character, love, and compassion of God, and then pray fervently that God—who owns the cattle on a thousand hills—will provide the financial resources for that ministry. Many churches are strangling because of leaders who believe that holding the purse strings is more important than ministry.

11. Must manage his own family well. This literally means, one who stands before his family—not above. He is a leader whom they are willing to follow because of his model character, not because he is a dictator. He stands before his family as a shepherd would stand before his sheep—to lead and to guide. He does not drive them or shout orders that have to be obeyed or foster paranoia or fear. They know his voice and know that his voice is for their benefit.

It is important for an elder to be a family man, and the primary testing ground of whether or not a man can manage God's family is whether or not he can manage his own. But "to manage" has been so often misunderstood. Many see the manger as a boss.

To manage properly is to bring whatever we are managing to its intended usefulness. To manage a family well is to allow that family the freedom to become the family that God wants. That is, a family where people can be loved and accepted when no one else will. A family is a place where forgiveness can happen. A family is a place where laughter can be experienced as well as tears. A family is a place where mistakes can happen without feeling like a total failure. A family is a place where we can grow from babes into mature adulthood.

To manage God's family then is to bring God's family to its intended purpose—that we become imitators of our heavenly Father, that we forgive one another, and that we be ministers of reconciliation.

Some have reduced managing God's family to just keeping on the doctrinal track, but there is far more for the maturing family of God—the growing process from infants to growing into the character of God with His priorities, His principles, and His behavior.

12. See that his children obey him with proper respect. The word for *children* here *(tekna)* normally refers to those who have not yet attained adulthood. It is inappropriate to evaluate the qualifications of an elder by the conduct of his grown children. There is too much in this world's environment that drains our children in the adult life to blame the parents for the decisions our adult children make. But a growing child who has no respect for his father is a reflection upon a father's personal and interpersonal skills at home.

It would be inappropriate for a person who does not have interpersonal skills to gain the love and respect from his children to be an elder-leader in the church. It would not be long before the children of God in the church would spot those deficiencies in interpersonal skills that would bring disrespect to the man. We would do as much damage to the man as we would to the church at large. Consequently, it is as much for the man's benefit that we allow him time to mature and sharpen his relating skills so that when he does become a leader in the church, he can do it with a sense of accomplishment and assurance and know that he is helping God's children become like Christ.

13. Not be a recent convert. This comes from the word from which we get our English word *neophyte.* As we would not allow a person just learning to walk to enter into an Olympic race, so we would not want a person who has just become a Christian to enter into an elder-leadership role. To do so would bring two disservices to him. It would add to his ego. All of us have enough of that. It is a rare person who is so selfless that he can handle honor without doing injury to his soul. The more immature we are, the more injury honor brings to our ego spirits. The second danger is that the person comes under the same judgment as did the devil. That is probably referring to seeking to take too much territory, having too much pride, and seeking to be more of a competitor to God

77

than God's companion. We can act like little gods, instead of acting like humble servants.

14. Have a good reputation with outsiders. It is interesting that it appears that more "outsiders" had good words for Jesus than some of the "inside" religious leaders. That is not because Jesus isolated himself from outsiders; He was known as a friend of publicans and sinners. But in those associations, He did not compromise His position, principles, or practices. They saw that He was honest, sincere, moral, and committed.

Have we ever asked outsiders their opinions of some men we may want to choose for elders? How about asking some non-Christians who do business with potential elders? How about asking some outsiders who may do recreational activities, such as bowling or golfing, with potential elders? Is a man's life with those who are outside the family the same as when he is with those who are inside the family? We are talking about consistency—the kind of consistency that would help attract the non-Christians to the Father rather than cause them to turn their backs from Him.

Below is a chart that will help us understand these characteristics and their relationship to an elder's function.

Characteristic	Its Meaning	Functions
Above reproach	Is not connected with immoral conduct	(This relates to all functions.)
Temperate	Is clear-minded, calm, well-balanced	Handling disputes, dealing with false teaching, discipline, counseling
Self-controlled	Is not given to temper tantrums not easily upset	Reconciling differences, handling criticism and disputes
Respectable	Has his morals in order, ethically honorable	Example-setter, teaching, counseling,

Hospitable	Loves strangers, friendly, warm, responsive	Following up on new people, accepting *all* people, shepherd/friend
Able to teach	Is skilled in teaching	Understanding the truth, communicating the truth effectively
Not given to drunkenness	Is not addicted to drink	Example-setter, handling stressful situations well
Not violent	Is not combative or belligerent	Handling disputes, teaching, promoting harmony
Gentle	Is controlled, patient, forbearing, kind	Spending time with grumblers and spiritual babes, handling disputes, allowing others time to grow to maturity
Not Quarrelsome	Does not battle, not contentious	Minister of reconciliation, handling disputes
Not a lover of money	Is not covetous or greedy, not stingy	Helping to meet others' material needs, positive planner of progress, visionary
Manages his own family well	Is a family leader whose children respect him and follow his teaching	Leader in God's family, caring for others with a loving, fatherly disposition
Not a recent convert	Is a mature Christian, not a beginner in the faith	Teaching, counseling, leading in worship, discipline
Well spoken of	Has a good reputation, known to have a good character	Representing the church to the community, example-setter

The above qualifications are given just as much to protect the person as to protect the church.

If a man does not have these characteristics, he will not function well as a biblical "overseer." Not functioning well will give rise to criticism, disrepute, and lack of respect by the people in the church.

The function of the overseer is to take personal responsibility for the various works of the ministry within the body for the good of the individual members. It is not *primarily* to attend board meetings, or to make administrative decisions. He is not a controller, a boss, a dictator, or someone through whom every decision has to go before anything can be done. He is a facilitator who allows people within the body to use their gifts for the good of the *whole* body.

Deacons (3:8-13)

The English word *deacon* comes from a Greek word that literally means servant (*diakonos)*. It underscores personal service rendered to another, usually with humility. It was first used to describe someone who waited tables for someone else. It was then expanded to describe all kinds of services rendered to another. In short, this person was known to be one who served.

The word is used twenty-nine times in the New Testament and refers to several different people:

1. Ones who seek greatness—Matthew 20:26; 23:11; Mark 9:35; 10:43.
2. Attendants at a banquet—Matthew 22:13; John 2:5, 9.
3. One who provided care to Jesus—John 12:26.
4. Governmental officials—Romans 13:4.
5. Jesus—Romans 15:8.
6. A woman—Romans 16:1.
7. Apostles—2 Corinthians 3:6; 6:4; Ephesians 3:7; Colossians 1:23, 25.
8. Preachers and teachers—1 Corinthians 3:5; 2 Corinthians 11:23; Ephesians 6:21; Colossians 1:7; 4:7; 1 Timothy 4:6.
9. Disguised workers of the devil—2 Corinthians 11:15.
10. One that promotes sin—Galatians 2:17.
11. A group of men chosen to serve with the elders—Philippians 1:1; 1 Timothy 3:8-13.

The verb form of this word is used primarily, but not exclusively, to describe taking care of someone's physical needs in a general way (Matthew 27:55; Mark 15:41; Luke 4:39; 8:3; John 12:26; Acts 19:22; 2 Timothy 1:18; Philemon 13; Hebrews 6:10). It is used to describe taking care of someone's specific needs: (a) providing or serving food (Matthew 8:15; 25:44; Mark 1:31; Luke 10:40; 12:37; 17:8; 22:26, 27; John 12:2; Acts 6:2); (b) providing friendship to a stranger (Matthew 25:44); (c) providing clothes for the naked (Matthew 25:44), (d) caring for the sick (Matthew 25:44), (e) providing care to prisoners (Matthew 25:44), (f) providing monetary relief (Romans 15:25; 2 Corinthians 8:19, 20).

The verb form also describes the activity of preaching (1 Peter 1:12; 4:10, 11), caring for spiritual needs, or a combination of physical and spiritual needs (Matthew 4:11; 20:28; Mark 1:13; 10:45; 2 Corinthians 3:3; 1 Peter 4:10, 11).

A study of the noun and verb forms suggests the deacons are leaders who work with the elders in meeting the needs of the people. The Bible is silent concerning their specific function. They are mentioned as a group only three times, and always in connection with elders (Philippians 1:1; 1 Timothy 3:8-13—twice).

Many people believe that the first deacons were the seven men selected by the congregation to care for widows who had no food provisions (Acts 6:1-6). Although we cannot be certain that they were the first literal "deacons," those who were called by that name, the situation of that selection probably gives us our best dynamic model for having deacons today.

The situation in Acts 6 was this: the apostles were not only leading, preaching, teaching, and praying, but were also involved in the benevolent work of caring for widows. When that benevolent work grew to such proportions that the apostles had little time left for the ministry of the Word and prayer, seven men were chosen to look after this need of the church body.

That principle should probably be followed today. Elders have the responsibility of the total shepherding activities of the church. However, they cannot do the total program themselves. Each Christian is to be a servant of Christ by helping to meet the needs of others. However, there comes a time in the life of a congregation that certain people need to be selected to insure that the needs of the body are taken care of. That initial group was the elders. As the need increased, another group needed to be selected as their assistants—the deacons.

Deacons are selected servants—not to take away the service from other members, but to help insure that the service is not

81

neglected. Deacons represent the whole congregation in specific kinds of services.

We have no clear teaching about how elders and deacons are to be selected. It is probably wise to select the deacons for a specified function rather than for a specified time; that is, selecting people who would be deacons of benevolence, counseling, absentee calling, hospital visitation, and the like. There should be no deacons if there are no specified services to be done.

To use the English word *deacon* for this function is not really to use a translation of the Greek word, but a carry-over of the Greek letters into English. It would be better to call these people "ministers" or "people-helpers." If we had been doing that through the years, then someone who was in the hospital who did not have the preacher visit could not say that his minister did not see him. For the truth would be that two or three ministers had come to visit, because these persons selected for this function would fulfill their responsibilities, freeing up the preacher for prayer and study of the Word.

There is no hint that this function of deacons is a policy-making function, as in administrative board meetings. They are simply servants meeting specific needs of the church body.

Because these ministers would have a variety of tasks in a variety of circumstances, working with both males and females in the midst of difficult times, it was important that they have the characteristics that would cause them to be respected, trusted, and not likely to fall into temptations. The same is true today. These special ministers will need to handle finances, confidences, and privileged information, such as specific needs of hurting people. It is important that they be trusted. Consequently, there are several characteristics that need to be considered in the selection:

(1) "Worthy of respect" (1 Timothy 3:8). This literally describes someone who is maintaining moral ethics, is stately and dignified, is serious-minded and does not take his responsibilities lightly.

(2) "Sincere" (1 Timothy 3:8). This term literally describes someone who does not have "divided words." He is not double-tongued. He can be trusted with what he says.

(3) "Not indulging in much wine" (1 Timothy 3:8). The deacon is someone who is not attached to or addicted to wine. He is not a drunkard.

(4) "Not pursuing dishonest gain" (1 Timothy 3:8). The deacon is content financially. Someone in this position could take advantage of people's emotions, particularly widows, and gain monetarily but dishonestly.

(5) "Must keep hold of the deep truths of the faith with a clear conscience" (1 Timothy 3:9). The deacon is someone who knows what he believes and stands on those beliefs. He must not be following every new fad; he will have his doctrinal anchors secure.

(6) "Must first be tested" (1 Timothy 3:10). That is, a deacon must be proven to have the above characteristics.

(7) "There is nothing against them" (1 Timothy 3:10). This does not mean they have never done anything wrong, but they are not presently being connected with immoral behavior. There is no current charge against their present style of living.

(8) "Their wives . . ." (1 Timothy 3:11). Their wives must have a good character. This deals with the inner life and includes the following characteristics:

a. "Worthy of respect." This literally refers to women who have godly attitudes in religious, family, and personal relationships. They are model examples that others can follow.

b. "Not malicious talkers." These women are not gossips; they do not pass on tidbits of information that they know about others.

c. "Temperate." They are alert, sensitive, and have themselves under control in both moral and doctrinal issues; they are well-balanced women.

d. "Trustworthy in everything." What they say you can trust, what they do you can trust; there are not "gray" areas in their lives.

Verse 11 can either refer to the wives of the deacons or women who themselves were female deacons. The word *wives* is literally *women,* and the word *their* is not in the Greek text, which literally reads, "In the same way, the women." There is no way to solve which it should be based on the Greek language. Each person will have to decide for himself whether he believes Paul was talking about the wives of the deacons or about women who served as deacons.

It is clear that Paul did refer to a woman with the very same term as that used to designate deacons (Romans 16:1). Many women of that time served Jesus (Luke 8:1-3), anointed Him, waited on Him in a hospitable way, and served the church (Romans 16).

Since the word *deacon* literally means a servant, it is unlikely that we should be in an argument as to whether or not women can serve in various capacities in the church. They have always been servants in and for the church.

If Paul was discussing women as female servants here, it seems strange that he did not refer to their marital status, as he did with the male deacons in the next verse.

For this reason, and since this section about women comes right in the middle of Paul's discussion concerning deacons, many think he was referring to the wives of the deacons. However, it is also strange—if Paul was referring to the wives of deacons— that he didn't say anything about the wives of the elders in verses 2-7.

If verse 11 does discuss female servants, perhaps one reason their marital status was not mentioned was that they were widows who were serving the church in various capacities, as is seen later on in 1 Timothy 5:9, 10. Perhaps the list of widows referred to there are the women who are referred to as selected servants here (1 Timothy 3:11).

(9) "The husband of but one wife" (1 Timothy 3:12). For a discussion of the meaning of this phrase, see its counterpart under the listing of the characteristics of elders (1 Timothy 3:2).

(10) "And must manage his children and his household well" (1 Timothy 3:12). For a discussion of this meaning, see the parallel discussion under the listing of the characteristics of elders (1 Timothy 3:4).

There are great values and rewards in serving the body of Christ with humility and without ulterior motives. That was the point Paul was stressing when he wrote, "Those who have served well gain an excellent standing and great assurance in their faith in Christ Jesus" (1 Timothy 3:13). Jesus made it clear that the greatest among mankind are those who serve the others (Matthew 20:25-28). Perhaps this reveals the meaning of Jesus' statement, "The first shall be last, and the last shall be first." Those who are unselfish servants of the church are usually the last to be served, to be appreciated, and to be honored. But they may be among the first to receive their rewards in Heaven. There may be a great reversal of who gets the greatest recognition when we all stand in the royal courts of Heaven.

The Foundation Upon Which the Church Is Built (3:14-16)

The instructions concerning elders and deacons, as well as the other instructions to Timothy, are essential because of what the church is. Paul mentioned three truths concerning the church in verses 14 and 15. The church is the family of God—God's household—and as a family, we need the modeling of people with keen interpersonal skills to help us grow up to be like the eternal Father, God himself.

No wonder the qualifications discussed above should first of all be tested in their family lives. It is one family with one Father and many different brothers and sisters. The many different brothers and sisters are in different phases of maturity. Some are spiritually immature as newborn babes. Some are in their "terrible two's" and very independent; they want to be in charge. Others are wrestling with what it means to be an adolescent in a world filled with temptations and need the modeling of good morals and the counsel of good sense.

Second, the people of God are called the "church of the living God." It is not the church of the elders, or of the deacons, or of the preacher, or of anyone else. It is the church of the living God. The word *church* means people who have been called out and have thus become an assembly, a gathering, or a fellowship. People have been called out from many different environments, lifestyles, and practices. The church has a wide range of differences, and people bring into the life of that assembly some of the baggage of their former habits, preferences, opinions, and feelings; but the unity within that gathering is there because of the living God. There is no other group that has such a membership that cuts across economical classes, educational backgrounds, age categories, employment, and professional activities.

The church is also referred to as the pillar and foundation of the truth. The truth here is Jesus himself. The main truth that the church should communicate is the person and the work of Jesus.

The church sometimes gets things turned around, majoring in minors and minoring in majors. The church of Ephesus had apparently been caught up in some of that. Godliness does not come by any other source than God himself and our identity with, and obedience to, Him. That's the confession by which Paul closed out this chapter (1 Timothy 3:16):

1. God "appeared in a body." He put on flesh—the flesh of Jesus.

2. He "was vindicated by the Spirit." The Spirit empowered that body and performed miracles through that body; the Spirit raised that body from the grave (Romans 8:11).
3. He "was seen by angels." Angels were actively involved in the life of Jesus. The angels announced His coming, proclaimed His birth, ministered to Jesus after the temptations, strengthened Him when He prayed in the garden, declared His resurrection to the women, and explained His ascension to the apostles. That makes Him above the angels; in fact, the writer of Hebrews makes it clear that He was above angels (Hebrews 1:4-14).
4. He "was preached among the nations." He was no fly-by-night imitation Messiah. People scattered all over the world were preaching about Him, especially those who were persecuted because they did.
5. He "was believed on in the world." People have put their trust in Him, and thus their lives have been changed.
6. He "was taken up in glory." He is at the right hand of the Father and is coming back for us.

This confession is another way to say that Christians should have "no creed but Christ." It is Christ who saves us and unites us. Anyone in Christ should recognize all others who are in Christ as their brothers and sisters in the family of God.

To the degree that we replace that confession with our pet doctrinal issues—whether those issues be a millennial position, eternal security, method of inspiration, women's role in the church, or some other—we begin to line up with those issues and bring disunity, disharmony, quarrels, and division into the body of Christ. It is possible for people to be converted to a doctrine rather than to Christ. No doctrine should have priority over the living and eternal Christ.

It is interesting that this confession comes at the end of the discussion about elders and deacons, for these men should be the leaders in focusing the church's attention upon the right issue—Jesus Christ. Elders and deacons who focus on hobby horses, individual decisions, systematic theologies, and/or various doctrinal issues are not serving as much as they are severing. They should help God's children sense a unity with all other of God's children, and apply that unity in love, peace, and acceptance.

It is Christ who unites. And what Christ has united, let no man put asunder.

CHAPTER SEVEN

An Attack and a Counter Attack

1 Timothy 4

The Attack (4:1-5)

Paul had just declared that the church is the "pillar and foundation of the truth" (1 Timothy 3:15). He also made it clear that the focus of that truth was in Jesus (1 Timothy 3:16). Anytime the "pillar and foundation of the truth" is being effective, you can be assured that there will be perverters and falsifiers of the truth ready to attack the church. The devil will see to that.

Although the New International Version does not indicate it, this chapter begins with the word *but* in the Greek. It is introducing a contrast to both the vessel of truth and the truth itself (1 Timothy 3:15, 16). In chapter 1, Paul spoke to Timothy about the legalists in the church. Here, he shared some of their hobbyhorses. Christ unites, but anytime we begin to specialize in issues other than Christ, we will plant the seeds for disunity. That was happening in the church at Ephesus.

The "later times" (1 Timothy 4:1) referred to that period of time between the first coming of Jesus and the second coming. Peter emphasized on the Day of Pentecost that the latter times or "last days" had already begun (Acts 2:16, 17). Between Satan's defeat on the cross and his final defeat at the coming again of Jesus, he is in a perpetual battle—trying to destroy the truth.

When Paul said "the Spirit clearly says," he was referring to the fact that he was inspired as an apostle (1 Corinthians 2:13). During this time, it seems that the Holy Spirit was warning the church through the apostles concerning those who would tear down the truth.

When Paul talked about people abandoning "the faith," he was not speaking about a denominational body of doctrine, as that term is often used today, but rather about faith in Jesus Christ himself.

Notice how people were abandoning Christ—by following "deceiving spirits and things taught by demons." The word *deceiving* literally means wandering. These teachings caused men to wander from the faith. Isn't it easy to wander from a pathway, from a goal, or from a plan? It can happen slowly, unintentionally, and without notice until the person who wanders is completely off the course. Notice that Paul talked about people wandering away from the faith by listening to meaningless talk (1 Timothy 1:6). In this section, he got specific as to what meaningless talk is.

That these false, demonic teachings had come through speakers is clear from verse 2. The demons used human instruments who were "hypocritical liars." The word *hypocritical* means play-acting. Evidently, these people appeared to be moral and religious, but their appearance was a mask. Jesus warned that we need to be aware of "wolves" who come "in sheep's clothing" (Matthew 7:15). Paul warned the elders at Ephesus that "wolves" would come; he even warned that some might come from within the eldership itself (Acts 20:29, 30).

These teachers did this with "seared" consciences (1 Timothy 4:2), which means consciences that were no longer sensitive to being corrected. This happens as a person continually refuses to be corrected by his/her conscience. The conscience becomes callous to the difference between right and wrong. How did that happen? They had listened to false teachers (1 Timothy 1:3-11), became attached to false teaching, and treated the false as true.

When Paul spoke about being seared "with a hot iron," he was picking up the terminology of branding. A branding was done to show the mark of ownership. The idea was to picture that those teachers belonged to Satan. Their activity was his; they were doing his bidding. As God is looking for men to do His work, so is Satan. Who owns us can be partly identified by the brand we carry, and the brand we carry is identifiable by the kinds of things we teach. Do they square with what God teaches?

Notice that not all of Satan's teachings lead us into immorality. Much of what he does leads us to morality, but morality that is divorced from Jesus as Lord and Savior. Many of the pagan religions have a handle on some type of morality; in fact, some are more strict than Christianity. Just because someone teaches morality does not mean he is from God. Here Satan's teaching has to do with asceticism—things *not* to do: not to marry and not to eat certain foods. Neither of those is wrong in itself, but both are wrong if they become our central doctrine to which salvation is tied.

Some probably forbade marriage under the umbrella that sexual expression for any reason was sin. (See 1 Corinthians 7:1-3.) Most pagan religions in that day (in many today, also) connected sexual intercourse with their pagan worship services; so the majority of people who grew up outside of Judaism and Christianity related sexual expression to pagan worship. Paul's teaching here did not solve the problem for Christians. In the second century, some heretics were teaching that if people were married, they had to get divorced in order to become Christians.

Abstaining from certain foods could be gleaned from the Old Testament, especially Leviticus 11. But to do that is to overlook the fact that Jesus himself cleansed all foods (Mark 7:18, 19—reinforced by Acts 10:9-16). It is our Deity, not our diet, that gives us salvation (Colossians 2:16—3:17).

The Counter Attack (4:6-16)

It is not possible to counter attack false teaching by simply being silent. Paul expected the leaders to point out to God's family the truths of the faith (1 Timothy 4: 6). Those truths have to do with grace, flexibility, and freedom. Paul again emphasized that we are not to get caught up in the "godless myths" and pet ideas that draw people away from the central truth of Christianity (1 Timothy 4:7). He outlined several activities for Timothy to undertake in the face of false teachers:

1. Point these things out to the brothers (1 Timothy 4:6).
2. Be properly nourished in the faith (1 Timothy 4:6).
3. Stay away from false teachers (1 Timothy 4:7).
4. Train yourself to be godly (1 Timothy 4:7).
5. Put your hope in God (1 Timothy 4:10).
6. "Command and teach these things" (1 Timothy 4:11).
7. "Set an example" in conduct (1 Timothy 4:12-16).
8. Maintain a Christlike relationship with others (1 Timothy 5:1-3).
9. Teach proper care and respect for other people in various categories (1 Timothy 5:4—6:2).

While certain ascetic practices may be valuable, godliness is far more valuable (1 Timothy 4:8). While the legalists emphasized one's relationship to things (like institutional marriage and food), Paul emphasized a relationship to God and to people. When Paul

89

spoke about godliness (1 Timothy 4:8), he went back to the "mystery of godliness," who is Jesus Christ (1 Timothy 3:16). And Jesus was certainly not an ascetic isolationist.

When Paul said that "godliness has value for all things" (1 Timothy 4:8), he was spotlighting the value of godliness to our mental, spiritual, and social health. We are just now discovering the dynamic relationship of God's teaching to our physical well-being. We now know there is great physical danger in retained guilt, anger, resentment, the refusal to forgive, impatience, and other sinful attitudes. We know the value of laughter to health. Remember the Proverb that says laughter is good medicine? We now know how faith helps our health. Doctors tell us that if a patient has no faith in them, the likelihood of that person's getting better is slim.

We now know the importance of good friendships in regard to our health. No wonder the Bible has a lot to say about our relationships with each other—in the context of friendships. The Bible talks about our relationship to our mates and to our children; it does not discuss these things as arbitrary commands from God to see whether we will obey. All of God's guidance through the Word is for our well-being. We know that people who have a stable network of family and friends supporting them are likely to live longer. Mortality rates of those who are religious is lower than for the non-religious.

God has called us to freedom. That freedom affects our health. We now know that people who are inflexible have a higher health risk than those who are flexible.

Godliness is not just a way to get to Heaven; it is a way to live better here on earth.

Our hope must be in a living God, not in a list of legalistic restrictions (1 Timothy 4:10). The Christian leader must model before his people an example of someone who is putting his faith in a living God and not in dead traditions. The example he sets must be in the following ways (1 Timothy 4:12-16):

1. "In speech"—in what he says and how he says it.
2. "In life"—in how he lives and why.
3. "In love"—in what he loves and why (also in what he hates, i.e., evil).
4. "In faith"—in the object of his trust.
5. "In purity"—he is not double-minded; has no ulterior motives.

6. In "the public reading of Scripture"—he is not ashamed of the Word of God (cf. Romans 1:16).
7. In "preaching and . . . teaching"—he is not ashamed to talk about God and apply His teachings to others.
8. In using his *charisma* ("gift")—he is not intimidated by opportunities that come his way.
9. In being "diligent"—he is not wishy-washy.
10. In "progress"—he is continually maturing into the likeness of Christ.

If Timothy neglected his gift (1 Timothy 4:14), his example and effectiveness would be weakened; so Paul encouraged him to not neglect his gift. Elsewhere, Paul encouraged Timothy to "fan into flame the gift of God" that was in him (2 Timothy 1:6). We cannot be precisely sure what that gift was, but it did relate to his ministry and call for boldness in his usage (2 Timothy 1:7).

Paul mentioned that the gift was given through a prophetic message when the body of elders laid their hands on him (1 Timothy 4:14). In 2 Timothy, however, he mentioned "the gift of God, which is in you through the laying on of my hands" (2 Timothy 1:6). There is no contradiction here. Probably in the midst of the assembly of elders, Paul received from God an inspired prophetic message that called Timothy into a special ministry, and God granted Timothy the equipment necessary for that ministry through the laying on of Paul's hands. The elders then laid their hands on Timothy, probably not for the purpose of granting Timothy the gift, but to commission Timothy to that ministry.

Another possibility is that Timothy received the gift through the partnership of the laying on of both the elders' hands and Paul's. A third possibility is that Timothy received two different gifts on two different occasions. One thing is certain—Paul, Timothy, and the elders knew what he meant; thus, Paul did not have to explain it fully.

Every Christian is gifted by God for some kind of ministry within the body for other people (Romans 12:4-8). God does not expect us to be involved in any ministry for which He has not equipped us. Any gift from God *(charisma)* is given to us for the purpose of service for others. It is for the good of all, not the identification of superiority or inferiority (1 Corinthians 12:7).

Our differences in gifts come from the one Lord (1 Corinthians 12:4-7). God's gifts will be as diverse as the needs of people, but they all are the work of the one and the same Spirit, and He gives to all as He determines (1 Corinthians 12:11). But after gifting us, God leaves the decision about whether or not we will use those gifts in His service. We can use them, abuse them, or lose them. We can express them or neglect them.

We must not be passive with God's gifts; we must develop them, fan them, and use them for God's work.

In short, Christian leaders are to watch both their lives and their doctrine closely (1 Timothy 4:16). That life is the life of Christ, and that doctrine is Jesus Christ himself. We have no creed but Christ. To substitute other creeds by demanding that people cave in to them for salvation is to make the cross of Christ null and void.

Isn't it time Christians knocked down the walls that divide them? Isn't it time we see that Christ and only Christ saves us?

I remember growing up with all the different restrictions concerning activities that supposedly prevented people from being saved—such as playing pool, roller skating, wearing make-up, and going to a movie. Today, some people expand these restrictions by dictating the kind of dress one can or cannot wear, the length of hair, whether a man can or cannot wear a beard, the day of the week that we must worship, the denomination we have to be a part of, the order of the worship service, whether or not one attends Sunday-night or Wednesday-night services, the kind of music sung or listened to, whether or not musical instruments can be used in worship, how often one takes the Lord's Supper, what one's millennial position should be, what one should think about the action of the Holy Spirit, and the list goes on.

While I am writing this chapter, a team is investigating a midair collision in the Los Angeles area. A pilot strayed off course and hit a jetliner full of people. What distracted that pilot? He was busy flying his plane; he was an executive and probably busily thinking about business decisions, or talking with his wife and daughter who were with him, or making plans about their outing in the mountains. He was busy doing good things. He was busy doing important things. But he strayed off course and wandered into an area where he should not have been.

Christians do the same thing when we get busy specializing in what we consider to be good things, important issues, pet doctrines, but take our eyes off the central focus point—Jesus. We stray off course; we get into areas where we should not be, and disaster strikes.

CHAPTER EIGHT

Proper Relationships

1 Timothy 5

First Timothy 5 deals with interpersonal relationships within the church. Most of the problems within the church come from inadequate relational skills, particularly when there are differences. Research has shown that only 15% of our problems, stress, and perplexities come because we do not have the correct knowledge. The remaining 85% comes because we do not relate to people well.

Paul had already stated that the goal of instruction is for love to come out of a pure heart, a good conscience, and a sincere faith (1 Timothy 1:5). Love means relationships; however, much of what was going on within that church was evidently weakening interpersonal relationships, such as the following:

1. A stress on myths and endless genealogies put a strain on relationships because some people would not be in the right family grouping.
2. A stress on legalism weakened relationships while heightening a judgmental attitude.
3. The neglect to pray for each other weakened sensitivity to others' needs.
4. An independent attitude of wives against husbands (or women against men) strained relationships.
5. The selection of unqualified elders would multiply negative relationships within the membership. For instance, a leader who was quarrelsome, a lover of money, violent, or not temperate would lead to negative interpersonal relationships. His actions and reactions would not reflect godliness.
6. The stress on asceticism built walls and made some to be in isolation.

Paul's emphasis on relationships at this point ties in with his stress on godliness (1 Timothy 4:8) in the following ways:

1. Godliness is expressed in relationships.
2. One specific way for youth to be respected (1 Timothy 4:12) is by the expression of healthy interpersonal relationships.
3. A way to be a model in speech, conduct, love, faith, and purity is to show those aspects in relationships.
4. A way to demonstrate progress in the Christian life (1 Timothy 4:12) is to show maturity in relationships.
5. A way to pay close attention to oneself (1 Timothy 4:16) is to extend oneself for the benefit of others in relationships.

This chapter deals with relationships across many different people categories:
1. Age categories—older and younger.
2. Sexual categories—male and female.
3. Social categories—widows with children, without children, older and younger widows.
4. Authority categories—elders.

The key concept in this chapter is found in verse 21, "Keep these instructions without partiality, and . . . do nothing out of favoritism." An umbrella idea that would cover this chapter could be the Golden Rule, "Do unto others as you would want them to do to you."

Relationship With the General Membership (5:1, 2)

In these two verses, Paul dealt with proper relationships across age categories (younger and older) and sexual categories (male and female). Many inscriptions in the first and second century praised those who had treated older people as parents and younger people as brothers and sisters.

What Not to Do

Proper relationships involve the negative as well as the positive—the *no*s as well as the *yes*es. A proper relationship with older persons (here older men) includes refraining from rebuking such persons. *Rebuking* refers to reprimanding harshly. It literally means giving a verbal blow.

Sometimes, it is easy for younger people to be verbally harsh with older people because they do not see older people as being open, flexible, contemporary, or progressive. Sometimes they think older people are stuck to "the way we have always done it." There are older people who are more secure in traditions and what was done in the past than in taking risks with innovations.

However, some (if not much) of what younger people see is really maturity in action. Some of the older people have already experimented with the ideas of the younger and have track records to show that some of those ideas are not workable.

But regardless of the reason that the older people may seem to be non-supportive, non-progressive, or non-growing, a rebuke is out of order. A better approach is to get to know those people, become their friends, do things with them, converse with them. Younger people should not build a wall between the young and the old in the church. We need one another. The younger need the maturity, the experience, and the practical advice of the older; and the older need the flexibility, energy, creativity, and freshness of the younger.

What to Do

(1) Treat older men as fathers. That means to treat them with respect, honor, and gratitude. The finest example of how to treat someone as a father is Jesus himself. Everything Jesus did was done to please His Father (John 8:29). There was unity between Him and His Father. Jesus understood His Father, communicated with His Father, and fellowshiped with His Father. That is what the younger need to do with the older—especially younger preachers relating to older men in the congregation.

(2) It is just as important to treat the younger men properly— as brothers. That means that we should not treat the younger as if they are inferior. We should not see ourselves as in authority while younger people are totally in submission. We should not see ourselves as wise, while younger people are "dumb." We should not see ourselves as right and younger people as wrong.

While older people may like the advice we just discussed about how they should be treated, now older people must listen to what Paul said about the treatment of younger people. Just as younger preachers should treat older men with respect, so older men should treat younger preachers with love, support, forgiveness, and protection.

It is too easy for men who have been in a church for a long time to feel as if they own the church rather than resting in the ownership of Christ. It is too easy for them to think that this is their territory and that a younger preacher is just a visitor who is passing through. It is too easy to treat a preacher, especially if he is younger, as a hired hand. It is too easy to think that with age comes automatic authority and wisdom. Whatever authority a person has is for the purpose of building up others, not for the purpose of tearing them down (2 Corinthians 13:10). If that is true for an apostle, it is certainly true for any older person in the church, regardless of his official status. For no one today has a higher status in the church than did the apostles in the first century.

(3) Christians should "treat ... older women as mothers and younger women as sisters, with absolute purity" (1 Timothy 5:2). *With absolute purity* means with no ulterior motives. No lust for money. No lust for sex. No lust for a power base. Some men wish to relate well to older women because they know that many of them hold the real influential base of a congregation. This is inappropriate.

Relating to women with absolute purity would stop any inappropriate motives. It would keep people from treating older women with favoritism in order to be named in their wills, or from ignoring them altogether. It would keep people from giving special attention to the younger women in order to get into their beds. That means watching what we say with our mouths, what we look at with our eyes, and what we do with our hands.

Our relationships must be filled with integrity and sincerity. We must seek to help the young and the old, the men and the women, to be more like Christ. It should not be to further our own selfish desires or causes.

Relationship With a Specific Category—Widows (5:3-16)

There are several principles that can be gleaned from this passage, but the most important is this: "Family members (i.e., children, grandchildren, or others) should care for the widows in their immediate or extended families." The children's responsibility to widows (and perhaps we could say to all aged parents) is transcultural. It was highly practiced among pagans at that time, as seen by the writings of Philo, Aristotle, Plato, and others. Aristotle said, "It should be thought in the matter of food we should help our parents before all others since we owe our nourishment to them. A man must starve before seeing his parents starve."

It is interesting that family relationships are still highly carried out in pagan cultures, particularly those that have a tribal situation. But sometimes family relationships and responsibilities are not carried out in Christian nations where we have nearly worshiped a sense of independence and personal success. Television and all other commercials feed this type of thinking—spend on self first, look out for number one, you will succeed by being self-oriented.

Other principles that might be cited basically come under this one. Some of those principles follow:

1. The church should not become a scapegoat for our lack of responsibility for our families.
2. Don't be duped by con-artists, regardless of how needy they may be. They may be truly alone (1 Timothy 5:5), truly committed (1 Timothy 5:5), truly aged (1 Timothy 5:9), have a good reputation (1 Timothy 5:10), and have good works (1 Timothy 5:10), but it is still the family members' responsibility first to care for the other family members.
3. Don't encourage dependency and thus restrict the young (1 Timothy 5:11-15). They have energies, dreams, desires, and abilities that should be lived out.
4. Idleness among the younger is devastating to purity, relationships, and responsibilities.

Widows Without Families (3, 5, 6)

In Judaism, widows received special care (Deuteronomy 10:18; 24:17; Isaiah 1:17; Luke 2:37). Christians continued such care (Acts 6:1; 9:39).

There seems to be two things at issue here with the widows without families. The church was providing special physical care for them, and there was a special ministry done by them, such as praying and visitation. Those who had no family were to receive special recognition (which meant financial support by the church) for the following reasons:

1. They were really in need (1 Timothy 5:3, 5).
2. They had no one else to take care of them—they were "left all alone" (1 Timothy 5:5).
3. They had put their hope in God, not in gadgets or even in family. Since the church is the household of God and indeed the dwelling place of God, to place hope in God is to place hope in the church.
4. They had taken their case to God in prayer (1 Timothy 5:5), and when God answers prayer, He often does it through His people—the church.
5. They did not live for pleasure (1 Timothy 5:6).

During the grief cycle, widows can begin to divert their attention for the purpose of feeling worthy and acceptable. They may spend their money in gadgets. They may begin to prioritize "me-ism." They may overindulge in spending, in immorality, in drink, in sexual experiences. A widow who is in that kind of life-style should not be helped financially by the church. When Paul said that such a widow was "dead even while she lives," he was referring to the fact that they were withdrawing from the abundant life full of joy, hope, and growth. Drowning one's sorrows in sensual living will only lead to misery and emptiness.

Verse 7 is a key verse for showing why Paul gave these instructions (that is, which widows to support and which not to support). The reason is so that no one may be open to blame. That "no one" includes older widows with no families and the younger widows with families. The older widows who need support could not be blamed for being freeloaders, because it is the church's responsibility to take care of them. The children, grandchildren, and relatives of widows could not be charged with being worse than unbelievers, for they would be taking care of their relatives. Remember that even "unbelievers" took care of the widowed in their communities in that day—and still today.

The church could not be blamed for wasting money by supporting widows who lived luxuriously for pleasure. The church could not be blamed for encouraging idleness by supporting the younger widows who had energy and time. The church could not be blamed for preventing younger widows from marrying by supporting them and perhaps using them in a special ministry that might prevent marriage. By not supporting younger women (which might have made it easier for them to become busybodies and gossips), it would prevent them from being blamed for inappropriate relationships within the body.

These instructions were given for the good of the women, not primarily to reduce the financial load of the church. It was not for budgeting reasons, but for the benefit of the members.

Widows With Families (4, 8)

Jesus sharply rebuked grown Pharisees who withdrew financial support from their parents with the excuse that the monies they had were already dedicated to the work of God (Matthew 15:1-9). That is like committing so much money to the Faith-Promise Program or to the church budget that we cannot help our aged parents financially. Jesus said that attitude and activity invalidates the Word of God. Such people may honor God with their lips, but their hearts are really far from Him.

Instructions for children, grandchildren, and others to care for the widows who are aged highlights the social need of keeping the generations together. In our highly mobile society, generations have grown apart from one another in proximity and in provisions, in relationships and in resources. For instance, in 1950, 50% of the homes in the United States had an additional adult living in—usually a grandparent. Today, fewer than 5% have that extended family situation.

We are all losers when we separate our relationships and care from the older generation. The youth do not benefit from the wisdom of the older, and the older do not gain the inspiration of the youth.

Paul made it clear that our religion must first of all be put into practice at home by caring for our families. We should be willing to repay parents and grandparents. After all, they brought us into the world and also brought us up. They cared for us, provided for us, loved us, forgave us, and educated us. They encouraged us to walk, to eat, to talk, and expand into the broader world. Our parents sacrificed significantly for us. They were willing to be inconvenienced for us. They took care of us when we were sick and in need; consequently, it is only proper that we do the same for them when they are in need.

For Christians to fail to do that is for them to turn their backs on something that even pagans understand is essential for proper relationships (1 Timothy 5:8). It is time for churches to begin to teach this responsibility in the junior-high department to the children as they are growing up. Children should look toward their middle-age life (when their own children are grown) expecting to be responsible for aged parents.

Children have no right to give this responsibility to the government or to the church. Neither the government or the church got up at 3 A.M. when we were infants and our bodies were hot with fever. Neither the government or the church watched us go to kindergarten. Neither the government or the church was there when we fell and got hurt. Neither the government or the church was there when the heart was crushed as a friendship fell apart. It was our parents. They were the ones who cared for us. They deserve our care in return.

A Certain Group of Widows (9, 10)

There was a special group of widows within the church that were included on a "list" (1 Timothy 5:9). This list was probably a service and support list—a list of those widows whom the church was supporting, but who were also rendering services. In one sense, their support could be seen as remuneration for their services. Those services might have included such things as visitation, caring for orphans, tutoring children, and counseling younger women.

By the second century, there was an established order of widows who would pray for people who were facing special temptations, care for sick women, and inform elders of the needs of women in the church body.

Today the church could have a special ministry of widows to do various services within the church:

1. Care for the physical facility.
2. Do tutoring for children having problems in school.
3. Visit invalids.
4. Visit people in the hospitals.
5. Hold special counseling sessions with younger women.
6. Serve as prayer warriors.
7. Write letters of encouragement to members of the church, to missionaries, and to those who have special joys or hurts.
8. Lead home Bible studies for women.
9. Telephone people in behalf of the church.
10. Manage a benevolent ministry—such as a thrift shop for lower income people.
11. Provide special counsel for the elders about the needs of women in our contemporary society.
12. Provide meals for special occasions and for older widowers, invalids, or others.
13. Provide free baby-sitting for younger married couples so they can have some time to be alone. Many young couples live far away from a family support base and need such help.
14. Perform special ministry to the grieved.

This special order of service for widows meant that certain characteristics must be a part of their life-style:

(1) She had to be at least sixty years old. She had to be mature. The maturity of character, however, is not indicated by age only. Thus, her maturity was to be evidenced as in the characteristics that follow.

(2) She must have been faithful to her husband. This is precisely the same phrase that we found in the characteristics of elders in 1 Timothy 3:2. It literally means "a one-man woman." It could refer to the following: a woman who never practiced polygamy, a woman who never experienced a divorce, a woman who never married after the death of her husband, a woman who never committed adultery, a woman who was committed to whatever husband she had. This latter seems to be the best choice here. There is no prohibition against a woman marrying after the death of her husband. A person who has gone through a divorce can be forgiven by God, and God expects us to forgive those whom He has forgiven.

Paul would certainly not suggest that a widow could never marry again and thus be disqualified for a special service in her later years, or he would not have advised the younger widows to get married (1 Timothy 5:14).

(3) She was well-known for her good deeds. She had a reputation of caring for others with unselfishness. Consequently, she had already been put to the test.

(4) She had brought up children. She knew the various passages a person goes through in life; she was able to counsel younger women; she was able to understand children's problems. This could also refer to those women in the first century who made it a practice to go to the marketplace, pick up the abandoned children, and raise them as their own.

(5) She showed hospitality. She was sensitive to the needs of strangers; she had no prejudices and thus was able to serve effectively in the church in the midst of a pluralistic society.

(6) She washed the feet of saints. No task was beneath her. She could reach out and minister in a very physical way. She was willing to do work of any type in order to meet the needs of those around her.

(7) She helped those in trouble. She was full of pity and mercy.

(8) She devoted herself to all kinds of good deeds. She was committed, unselfish, showed unconditional love ("all kinds"), and knew what needed to be done to be the most beneficial. She had her priorities in the right place.

Young Widows (11-15)

Paul was not prejudiced against younger widows, but he was being practical; he understood their needs, desires, and potential problems. These widows could have been middle-aged or those who were "new" widows (had just recently lost their husbands). The word *younger* is built from the Greek root word for "new" *(neos)*.

"Do not put them on such a list"—Paul was not indicating that the church should not financially help young widows, especially if they had no families. In fact, many young widows had no families who would help them: their children were too young to help financially, they had no grandchildren to help, and some had no brothers and sisters who could help. These widows in our contemporary culture are often the most alone. The church must help in these instances.

Since this "list" was probably a service-support list, it would have required that these widows make a commitment of service to the church. Evidently that commitment involved a vow that they would not marry again; they would spend the rest of their lives in this kind of "full-time" service. That is why there was the age requirement of sixty years and older. It is important to note that being sixty years old in the first century was far older than being sixty years old today in the United States.

We should not be legalistic about the age requirement today. What seems to be the issue is the health, life expectancy, and energies of women.

Paul did not want to put the younger widows on the list because a lifetime vow of remaining unmarried to serve in the church would result in the following:

1. It would violate their sensual desires. Nothing is wrong with sexual desires. They are one of God's clues that a person has the *charisma* for marriage (1 Corinthians 7:7).

2. It would hinder their desire for marriage, the normal outgrowth of having sexual desires.

3. They would be guilty of breaking a lifetime pledge if they married (1 Timothy 5:12). Paul did not want to put that burden upon the younger widows.

4. It would wrongly direct their energies. They would have extra time to spend in fruitless and unfulfilling activities (1 Timothy 5:13). Too much free time can cause us to be involved in things we normally would not do. These younger women would have enough energy to do the service work and have extra time left over. They would be tempted to go from house to house, passing on gossipy tidbits that they heard, becoming busybodies

(this literally means "to go around work"), emphasizing the social rather than the spiritual, being busy but not productive. They would say things that should not be said; idle time leads to idle talk. We are told in Proverbs that when we talk too much, we will hurt others as well as ourselves.

Because of these reasons, Paul encouraged the younger widows to marry, to have children, to manage their homes, and to give the enemy no opportunity for slander (1 Timothy 5:14). This would not mean that a widow has to marry again for the purpose of having children. Paul was simply saying that they did not have to remain widows the rest of their lives. They could look forward to another wholesome family life.

The younger widows did not have to follow in the footsteps of the older widows by engaging themselves in service to the church that would prevent another marriage. Paul was freeing them up.

The summary statement concerning widows is found in 1 Timothy 5:16. It is obvious that we have a responsibility to the widows in our families, both immediate and extended. The church also has a responsibility, but she should be liberated to help those who are truly in need—those who have no one who can help. The church can be partners with the families in helping every widow in the community. To the degree that Christian family members and the church do *not* do it in the name of Christ, community agencies will do it on behalf of some other name.

Relationship With Church Leaders (5:17-25)

The devil will do anything he can to bring the church to a place of ineffectiveness. One of his slickest schemes is to cause distrust to be planted in the minds of people against their leaders. That happened to Jesus. Satan caused people to believe that Jesus was a blasphemer, a liar, and a fake. He also caused people to make false charges against the apostles, like Peter and Paul. To weaken trust in the leadership is to plant seeds for deterioration within the church (in interpersonal relationships) and outside the church— that is, the effectiveness of the church in the community.

Thus, we must learn and consider how to relate properly to the leaders of the church. There are several principles outlined in this passage:
1. Respect them (1 Timothy 5:17).
2. Pay them financially (1 Timothy 5:17, 18).
3. Protect them (1 Timothy 5:19).

4. Purify them when necessary (1 Timothy 5:20).
5. Do not choose them too quickly (1 Timothy 5:22).
6. Encourage them to take care of their physical bodies (1 Timothy 5:23).
7. The leadership will reap what they sow and will be known by their fruit (1 Timothy 5:24, 25).

Respecting and Paying Our Leaders (17, 18)

Paul talked about giving "double honor" to the elders "who direct the affairs of the church well." This translation is somewhat misleading. It gives us the idea that these elders are the dictators who tell others what to do, when to do it, and how to do it.

The Greek word used here is used elsewhere in the New Testament to describe those who help others (Romans 16:1—about Phoebe), those who have the gift of leadership (Romans 12:8), those who work hard (1 Thessalonians 5:12), those who "devote themselves" to doing good (Titus 3:8, 14). The literal meaning is "someone who stands before others." The elders stand before others as model servant-leaders who reach out to help people by devoting themselves to doing good for others. They are the ones who look upon people for the purpose of looking after them.

Such men are "worthy of double honor." The word *honor* was sometimes used to refer to financial help (Matthew 15:2-5) and was also used that way when talking about widows (1 Timothy 5:3, where the word *recognition* is the same as the word here translated "honor"). Giving honor certainly does include paying those elders who are giving themselves significantly to meeting the needs of others. The more an elder gives of himself, the more time is taken away from his wage-earning activities. If we ask a man to give so much time that it cuts into his wage-earning activities, then we need to supplement or provide the funds he needs to support his family.

This was especially true of those who work at preaching and teaching. Notice that "preaching and teaching" was called a "work." The Greek word for *work* stresses wearisome, toilsome, fatiguing labor. Isn't it time that we understood that preaching and teaching are indeed hard work? Some people look at the preacher as being on "easy street." Some have been known to disrespect their preacher by improper pay, thinking he does not work hard. Preparing and doing an effective job in the preaching ministry is time-consuming and energy-draining.

Evidently, the preachers in the Ephesian church were also elders. It can be wise in a practical sense to select the pulpit preacher as an elder if he also fulfills the necessary qualifications. Paul used an Old Testament verse to communicate that anyone is worthy of his wages, including the ox who is treading grain. Elsewhere, he said that we do not expect soldiers and farmers to work without remuneration; neither should we expect preachers to do so. He made it clear that he who sows spiritual seed should be able to reap a material harvest (monetary return) from that labor. He said, "The Lord has commanded that those who preach the gospel should receive their living from the gospel" (1 Corinthians 9:7-14).

It is a wise church that will free up one or more persons to be available at any time to minister to the needs of people and to motivate others to do so. We cannot expect a person who works on an assembly line and commutes two hours each day to have a lot of time or energy to do church-related work. Someone needs to be on call when a death occurs, when counseling is needed, when a person is considering suicide, or when a child has run away. We cannot expect to call a man away from his job to meet such needs. Most supervisors may allow it once, but not repeatedly.

It is a ministry of the body of Christ to free people from their career responsibilities so they can concentrate upon the needs of the congregation. It is, in effect, saying, "We are freeing you from plowing the fields, working on the assembly line, selling products, or running an office to share and serve our congregation. Paying the preacher or elder does not let the rest of us off the hook, however. We must all be involved in the church's ministry to whatever degree we can in our present life situations.

To pay the preacher or elder is Biblical, but to treat him as a temporary hired hand, as someone inferior, or someone whom we will keep poor is not Biblical. May those who are involved in preaching and teaching not feel guilty because they are paid. May those who pay them not be stingy.

Protecting Our Leaders (19)

The unity, strength, and progress of a church body can be seriously hurt by gossip and unfounded accusations. Unless there are actual witnesses, no one should let any accusation about an elder (or any other leader) carry weight. We are not to go on witch hunts. False accusations put Jesus on the cross. May the day of crucifixions be over.

Purifying the Leaders (20)

On the other hand, those who have really sinned need to be brought to accountability for the purpose of causing them to repent and for the purpose of showing others that sin is not taken lightly among the leadership. However, we need to be cautious, lest we allow accusations to be brought because of one sin. The tense of the verb form "sin" in this verse emphasizes continuous, habitual sin.

We must understand that all leaders are vulnerable and open to yielding to temptation. This does not mean it is right, but it does mean that we must quit thinking that our leaders are perfect and will not sin. Our leaders are not superhuman, but just human. If an elder forgets that, he will fail to buffet his body daily, as Paul mentioned he had to do (1 Corinthians 9:27). And if we forget that, we can lose confidence in the church leaders when they do not live up to our expectations in a particular situation. We could use that man's sin as an excuse for not being involved in God's work.

At the same time, we must not be involved in cover-ups when a leader is involved in continuous sin. The elder who sins must become aware of his wrong in order to repent, and the others must hold him accountable and give him warning. That "warning" also involves the other elders realizing that they too have feet of clay and can be duped by the devil and his crowd.

What it means to rebuke him "publicly" is problematic. It could mean one of the following:
1. To rebuke him in front of the entire congregation.
2. To rebuke him before those against whom he has sinned.
3. To rebuke him in front of the other elders.
I believe the third choice seems to fit the context, for it was to be done "so that the others may take warning." The "others" most likely means the other elders.

Doing this is tough in the family of God, because we do not want to hurt anyone. The purpose is to benefit all. Consequently, the charge needs to be kept "without partiality" and without "favoritism" (1 Timothy 5:21). It is done to help the elder who sins as well as the others who are in leadership.

Using Caution When Selecting Leaders (22)

One of the ways to prevent having to have public rebukes often is to select the elders carefully. If one is going to *rebuke* without partiality and favoritism, he needs to *select* without partiality and favoritism. That means we should not select elders on a popularity vote or simply because they are likable. Elders (as well as deacons) must be chosen carefully out of the qualifications listed in chapter 3.

If we choose a man quickly who does not fulfill the qualifications, we are setting him up for moral failures. Review the characteristics that the elders should have and meditate upon what failures they could have because they did not have the characteristics.

Characteristic	Failure if Missing
1) Faithful to his wife	Adultery
2) Not a lover of money	Embezzlement, greed, dishonesty
3) Not given to much wine	Drunkenness
4) Not quarrelsome	False charges, disharmony
5) Apt to teach	False doctrines
6) Temperate, self-control	Gluttony, temper tantrums

Physical Fitness for Leaders (23)

Timothy evidently had stomach problems and frequent illnesses. After telling Timothy to "keep yourself pure," Paul probably remembered that Timothy had adopted total abstinence as a part of his purity; so he qualified purity in such a way that made it clear that total abstinence is not necessarily a part of it. It may be that some false teachers had made total abstinence a big issue, as in the other aspects of asceticism (1 Timothy 3:4).

Wine used for medical reasons would not violate purity. Hippocrites, father of medicine, wrote about the significance of moderate doses of wine for a patient whose stomach was endangered by the use of water alone. Wine was listed as a type of medicine. It is as medicine that Paul gave his advice. Perhaps that was why he did not demand total abstinence from wine as the characteristic of an elder or deacon.

To suggest that this verse puts a stamp of approval on social drinking is as much out of context as to suggest that penicillin parties are appropriate because penicillin is a medicine. On the other hand, we are on shaky ground Biblically to demand total abstinence in regard to wine.

Wine was seen in the Old Testament as a blessing from God (Deuteronomy 7:12, 13). It was one of the offerings to be given to God (Deuteronomy 14:22, 23; 18:4). Lack of wine was seen as a punishment from God, while new wine was seen as a reward for honoring God (Proverbs 3:9, 10; Jeremiah 48:32, 33). The gathering of wine was seen as a celebration (Deuteronomy 16:13). Wine was given as a gift to the needy (Deuteronomy 15:14). Abstinence was a special vow that some people took (Numbers 6:1-7). This verse under discussion gives us neither liberty for condemnation nor a license for drunkenness.

A Leader Reaps What He Sows (24, 25)

A leader will not be able to hide his sins (1 Timothy 5:24) or his good deeds (1 Timothy 5:25). Both sins and good deeds will be made evident here and on the Day of Judgment. Sin will eventually catch up with us in this life and certainly reveal who we are before the throne of God. And good works will have an evident manifestation that benefits others here and will produce rewards for those who do them.

We cannot hide from God or from people. Neither are dumb or blind. Man's wrongs and rights are seen by those around him and by God above. These wrongs and rights relate to the rest of this chapter. What we do concerning our elderly parents will be known here and in Heaven. What we do concerning our leaders in the church (our treatment of them, our payment of them, our accusations about them, our forgiveness of them) will be known both here and in Heaven. How we use or misuse wine will be known here and in Heaven.

No man is an island. We live with God, for God, and in the presence of God. If we are not practicing the advice of this chapter, we need to repent now. God takes our relationships seriously, and so should we.

CHAPTER NINE

Stand Up for Christ

1 Timothy 6

In this chapter of 1 Timothy, Paul dealt with two environments in which it was not easy to stand up for Christ but was essential to do so—at work and when facing false doctrine (1 Timothy 6:1-10). He then gave Timothy the marching orders to fight the good fight in those environments.

Stand Up for Christ in the Workplace (6:1, 2)

Half of the Roman Empire was made up of slaves in Paul's day. But most of them were not slaves the way we think of slavery (the type of slavery that was prevalent prior to the Civil War in the United States). Many slaves were educated and cultured; thus some of the most competent professions in that day were held by slaves—lawyers, doctors, and teachers, to name a few.

Many slaves had more education than their masters. The masters usually treated such slaves very well and gave them many rights; of course, there were some masters who insisted on keeping their superior stance and treated their slaves with disrespect.

When the Master (or Employer) Is a Non-Christian (1)

The employee-employer relationship today is the closest application to what Paul was teaching. It is tough for a Christian to work for a non-Christian when the employer expresses pagan perspectives and values. Isn't it easy to criticize that employer, refuse to carry out one's work, and rebel? However, the Christian is to work for the non-Christian in such a way that God's name and the Christian teaching are not slandered.

Non-Christian employers may not read the Bible, go to church, attend Christian concerts, or listen to the Christian radio stations, but they see a sermon in the life-style of the Christian. The Christian becomes God's messenger to the (2 Corinthians 3:3).

The Christian is to treat his employer with "full respect" (1 Timothy 6:1). That includes doing an honest day's work, going the "second mile," not backbiting, helping other employees develop a team spirit, being positive, not coming in late or leaving early or taking longer breaks or lunch hours than permitted. In short, "full respect" means to allow the fruit of the Spirit to be seen in the work relationships—love, joy, peace, patience, kindness, goodness, faithfulness, gentleness, and self-control.

When the Employer Is a Christian (2)

Some Christian employers observe that their worst workers are Christian employees, especially those that belong to the same church. There seems to be a tendency for them to take advantage of their Christian employer, because their employer knows them well and is a Christian.

There can be the tendency to allow the equality of church membership to blur the chain of command at the place of employment. In fact, sometimes roles are reversed at work. An employee may be the chairman of a church committee of which his employer is a member, but at work, the employer is "chairman."

Working for a Christian brother gives no ground for showing less respect to him. In fact, a Christian employee should be more willing to go the "second mile," to work overtime or give extra energy for the Christian brother because he is a brother—it is a *family* relationship.

All of us need to understand better the significance of saying "our" Father in our prayers. There is an "ourness" in our Christian walk that cuts across all human categories. If we take seriously that God is "our" Father, then we must treat His other children as He treats them. The way we treat another Christian at church or at work is, in essence, the way we are treating God.

A Christian employee cannot replace the "our" concept with the "me" concept when working for a Christian employer. Doesn't that make sense? Our good work for a Christian employer can allow him to benefit: he may have less stress and more energy, the product may be better, profits may increase, and he may be able to give more time and money to kingdom work.

Stand Up for Christ Against False Doctrine (6:3-10)

Paul ended his letter with the same emphasis with which he began it—against false teachings (1 Timothy 1:3-11).

False doctrines can be identified in one of two ways:

1. They contradict Jesus, and thus weaken a person's faith in Jesus—the rootage.
2. They approve (and may encourage) ungodliness and a lack of holiness in conduct and thus weaken a person's life in Jesus—the fruitage.

In chapter 1, Paul talked about the *content* of false teaching—legalism over against grace; but here Paul included *attitudes* and *motives* that accompany false doctrine: conceit, ignorance, an unhealthy interest in controversy, and—especially—greed, being motivated by material gain.

(1) Conceit. A person who is puffed up is full of his own self-importance. He is not open to learn from others.

(2) Ignorance. Paul said such a teacher "understands nothing" (1 Timothy 6:4). He may know many facts, but he does not understand what he knows. Some people know the data but don't know what "stands under" that data. It is one thing to memorize systems in doctrine and theology; it is another to understand the grace of God and the attitude of Jesus Christ. Conceit blocks understanding.

(3) An unhealthy interest in controversies and arguments. This is natural for someone who is conceited. *Unhealthy* literally means a sickness. This person is hooked on word wars. Why? Because winning word wars adds to his ego. Haven't we all known someone like that? Don't we all know those who raise questions over nit-picky things? They don't want to come to any understanding; they would rather show off their great intellects. Their heads are bigger than their hearts.

Such actions and attitudes hinder the healthy body life of the church. Instead, the following results: envy, quarreling, malicious talk, evil suspicions, and constant friction.

Envy means ill will toward another person. *Quarreling* comes about because of sick attitudes toward others; *malicious talk* designates the use of ill words about others; *evil suspicions* are sick thoughts about others. Add all these up, and the result is a total sickness—a corrupt mind. And it all begins with conceit. No wonder God said, "Pride goes before a fall."

Doesn't this give us practical reasons for the qualifications of the elders in 1 Timothy 3? It is not only for the good of the congregation, but also for the elder that he have those qualifications. And that is why Paul did not want Timothy to be too quick about laying hands on people (1 Timothy 5:22). Is it possible that the teachers in 1 Timothy 1:3-11 and 4:2, 3 were men who had been made elders too quickly and had become conceited? If these teachers were not elders, then at least we know that what happened to them could happen to elders who were selected too soon.

Look at the following chart. Notice how some of the qualifications of the elders stand opposite to these attitudes:

Bad Attitudes	Qualifications of Elders
Hooked on word wars	Apt to teach
Envy	Uncontentious
Quarreling	Not pugnacious
Malicious talk	Gentle
Evil suspicions	Hospitable, temperate

(4) Motivated by material gain. Religious activities were being used to line the pockets of the teachers. When teachers/speakers notice that they are getting a following, it is a real temptation to take financial advantage of it. Some do it by charging a "minimum" for each talk (which is usually extremely high). Some continue to stay on a certain topic because that is what the hearers want to hear and will support.

Although Paul mentioned the false motivation of gain, he did not want to leave the impression that godliness has no gain to it. So he said, "Godliness with contentment is great gain" (1 Timothy 6:6). *Contentment* means freedom from worrying about external circumstances and refers to satisfaction with the basics of life—food and clothing (1 Timothy 6:8).

It includes the knowledge that "we brought nothing into the world, and we can take nothing out of it" (1 Timothy 6:7). Contentment understands that we are all a vapor and that the mortality rate for all of us is 100%. That means we will have to let go of all we have accumulated soon, but God is preparing Heaven and its treasure for us—great gain. Godliness with contentment can better our attitudes and improve our health—great gain.

Unless we are content, we may fall into many snares, such as the following:

1. We may get mad because we are in Christian service but not making as much money or succeeding as well financially as others.

112

2. We may blame God for set-backs.
3. We may be filled with jealousy of others who have more.
4. We may fail to rejoice in the promotions and the benefits that come to our brothers or sisters in Christ.
5. We may have marital strife.
6. We may alter our motives.
7. We may use inappropriate methods.
8. We may change our priorities.

The opposite of contentment is seen in the person who is obsessed with getting rich (1 Timothy 6:9). That desire is a trap with all sorts of alluring bait. The bait is disguised and deceptive. A person did not intend to get caught in the trap; he *fell* into it.

These desires "plunge men into ruin and destruction" because they are based on a *love* of money that is "a root of all kinds of evil." Notice that it is *a root*, not *the root*. Money itself is not evil, but the love of money is a root that produces many kinds of fruit—drugs, prostitution, homosexuality, pornography, murder, lying, envy, sexual perversions, stealing, arson, divorce and remarriage, embezzlement, and many more.

Yet the depth of destruction is not seen in those evils alone, but by the decision to walk away from Christianity, which follows. Because of the love of money, the pull it has on our desires, and the priority it becomes, some have "wandered from the faith and pierced themselves with many griefs" (1 Timothy 6:10).

Just what constitutes the love of money? The Greek word translated "love" here is the word that emphasizes affection. A person has a love of money when the object of his affection is money. It is one thing to *have* money, but it is another for it to become the object of our affection.

This can happen to a person who has little or much. It is not the problem of just the rich. No one is richer than God, but He does not have an affection for those riches. Some of God's greatest people in the Bible were extremely wealthy—Abraham, David, Solomon, and Job. Some of Jesus' friends were evidently quite wealthy—Matthew, Joseph of Arimathea, and probably Mary, Martha, and Lazarus. Many of the early converts in Christianity were wealthy enough to sell extra real estate in order to help the poor, while still maintaining their own homes. So the issue is not how much or how little a person has, but what are his attitudes about what he has. It is quite possible for a very poor person to make money the object of his affection as well as the rich.

113

The object of the affection is not just in money *per se,* but in all that accompanies having money—recognition, power, status, independence, prestige, influence, services, gadgets, luxuries, travel, and a select circle of acquaintances.

Whatever becomes the object of our affection determines our priorities. But it is not wealth or lack of it that determines our priorities. We read a lot about the "patience" of Job when he lost his riches, his family, and his health. But prior to adequately understanding his patience, we need to understand his priority. The reason he could be patient with those losses was because his priority was higher than any or all of that. His priority was serving and pleasing God. The object of his affection was God. He knew that only God was everlasting. Consequently, he was wise enough not to put his hope in the uncertainty of wealth (1 Timothy 6:17) or in the temporary relationship with family and health.

There is a great difference between the desire to become rich and the desire to serve God with riches. The desire to become rich focuses our affection onto the riches, not God. It was about this type of person that Jesus said, "It is hard for a rich man to enter the kingdom of heaven" (Matthew 19:23). It was to the person who put his security in riches that Jesus said, "Woe to you who are rich, for you have already received your comfort" (Luke 6:24). That is the reason one of the richest and wisest men who ever lived on earth wrote, "Whoever trusts in his riches will fall" (Proverbs 11:28).

It is certainly okay to be rich, but we are told by God, who understands our affection well, that the rich man should not boast in his riches (Jeremiah 9:23). Jesus made it clear that riches are deceitful (Mark 4:19). They are deceitful concerning what is real security, what is real value, what is real purpose in living, what is really meaningful, and what will be really lasting after we are gone.

So the real dangers of having money as the object of our affection is not in any specific list of sins, but in the fact that such misplaced affection will cause us to wander from the faith and we will have much grief because of evil—evil that taints our priorities, our values, and perspectives—the evil that grows within a person when riches become what we love. The bottom line is simply this—are we building God's kingdom or our own? Only God's kingdom will last. And only God's kingdom will give us joy.

Fight the Good Fight (6:11-16)

Standing up for Christ involves taking stands. We must take a stand for Christ at our places of work, when facing false doctrine, and when surrounded by the lure of monetary gain. If we don't stand for Christ, we might fall for cash. If we don't stand for Emmanuel, we might fall for error. If we don't stand for the Divine, we might fall for the devil.

Paul used many military terms in this passage, such as *flee, pursue, fight, take hold, charge,* and *command*. Christians are to be soldiers, but some are A.W.O.L. (away without official leave). Some remain in the barracks. Some stay in boot camp. Some never advance to the front lines. Some are deserters. Some are cowards. Some have taken early retirement.

When Paul said, "Flee from all this" (1 Timothy 6:11), he was calling for Timothy to take on new armor, to put on a new uniform, to get new orders, and quit living as if he was still a civilian. In his second letter to Timothy, he elaborated on what he meant here. He said, "No one serving as a soldier gets involved in civilian affairs" (2 Timothy 2:4).

It is interesting to note that the Latin word for pagan *(pagani)* was originally used to describe a civilian—somebody who had not entered into the military for battle. God sees pagans as those people who have not joined Jesus' cause. Instead of *fighting* the enemy (the devil), they are on his side. But a Christian flees all of this; we desert the devil's cause. We become "turncoats." That is what repentance is all about. True repentance is to deny the devil as our commander in chief and affirm that we are going to march under a new banner with a new commander in chief in a new army. Instead of pursuing unrighteousness in the devil's army, we are now pursuing "righteousness" (right relationships), "godliness" (which includes God's life-style), "faith" (which includes trusting in a new commander in chief), "love" (which is our adherence to our commander in chief, "endurance" (which means we are not going to desert), and "gentleness" (which means we remain under the control of Christlikeness).

With those kind of characteristics, we are soldiers ready to fight the good fight of faith. There is a bad fight and a good fight. The bad fight includes fighting one another over nonessential doctrinal issues that so easily divide Christians. The good fight is the fight of faith. The fight of faith is one thing and one thing only—trusting in Jesus Christ. He is our center, our commander in chief; He unites us. He is *the* doctrine. To take hold of Jesus is to "take hold of eternal life to which you were called when you made your good confession in the presence of witnesses" (1 Timothy 6:12). What makes the confession "good" is the content of our confession—we are confessing Jesus Christ.

Some people have misunderstood what makes the confession "good." They think it is an exact formula that has to be said. But there is no set order of words. Jesus himself testified the good confession before Pontius Pilate, but Jesus used no memorized arrangement of words. He simply testified before Pilate that God was the Father and He himself was God's Son.

Matthew records Peter's good confession with a certain set of words, "You are the Christ, the Son of the living God" (Matthew 16:16). But when Mark quotes Peter, he does not use the same exact words: "Peter answered, 'You are the Christ' " (Mark 8:29). Luke uses still another phrase: "Peter answered, 'The Christ of God' " (Luke 9:20).

Thomas simply said, "My Lord and my God!" (John 20:28). When Peter preached on the Day of Pentecost, he told the people about the good confession when he said, "God has made this Jesus, whom you crucified, both Lord and Christ" (Acts 2:36). Upon that testimony, 3,000 people became Christians. We must quit arguing and fussing about the exact wording. To do so is to slip into the problem of 1 Timothy 6:3-5.

Paul lifted up the majesty of God in 1 Timothy 6:15, 16. As he did that, he used revolutionary words about God. At that time, Caesar of Rome was claiming to be "God," "Lord," "Savior," and "immortal." While we read these verses as a very neutral confession, it was the kind of confession that caused Christians to lose their lives in that day. This confession stood against Caesar by affirming that no human being is Lord; God is the *"only* Ruler"; He is the King over all kings. He is the Lord of all and over all, including the political leaders in Rome. He alone is immortal. No Roman Caesar had that longevity. To God and to God only belong honor and might forever.

If we think this confession was just nice neutral words, try to affirm that in a science or philosophy class at a state university.

Command the Good Life (6:17-19)

The good fight can be lost unless God's fighters put on the whole armor of God and allow God to use their possessions.

Riches can easily create misplaced hope. We can hope in the riches, but they are temporary. We must hope in God, who is eternal.

Every Christian soldier should be willing to be rich not only in goods, but also in good deeds. He is to be rich in generosity and willingness to share with others in need. There are three possible attitudes one can take about riches:

1. What is mine is mine and I will keep it.
2. What is yours is mine and I will take it.
3. What is mine is God's, and I will share it when there is need.

Those who invest their riches for the priorities of the kingdom have invested for dividends beyond any human imagination. They are investing in "treasure for themselves as a firm foundation for the coming age, so that they may take hold of life that is truly life" (1 Timothy 6:19).

Someone has said that the wisest investors are those who invest in what outlasts life. Investing in kingdom work outlasts life on earth. Of course, Paul was not saying that we cannot use our money for things other than kingdom work. But we are not to be stingy. We are not to hoard what we have while kingdom work is begging. We are not to get angry every time we receive another request for our generosity.

Isn't it interesting that many people will commit themselves to make house payments for thirty years, which will total three or four times the price of the house, but get angry if the church asks for a three-year commitment to a building program? Isn't it interesting that some people will spend $10,000 to $20,000 every four years for an automobile that is heading to the junkyard, but have never yet spent that kind of money for kingdom work over the same period of time? What would happen if every Christian made a commitment never again to spend more money on car payments than on kingdom work?

Guard the Trust (6:20, 21)

Every person who has spent much time in the military service knows what it means to be on guard duty. Each guard is assigned a certain area to keep safe, secure, and protected. Christian soldiers have also been given an area. We are to guard "the faith." That does not mean we are to guard our denomination, our opinions, our pet hobbyhorses, our arguments, or our controversies. But we are to guard the essential focus of the Christian's faith—

Jesus Christ. We are to allow no teaching, no attitudes, and no doctrines to become more important than Jesus. None of that should block a person's view from seeing Jesus.

Some people have been converted to a millennial position, or to a baptismal position, or to an eternal security position, or to a free will position who have not been converted to Jesus. They place their salvation in an "extra"—not the essential, Jesus. Consequently, their knowledge is in intellectual pursuits, systematic theologies, or doctrinal outlines and schemes. They will spend time in chatter, controversy, and debates about what they think is important knowledge. Some have been so hooked on those side trips that they have indeed "wandered from the faith."

In Paul's day, the side trip was centered largely in legalism. The Jews wanted the Christians to get back to the law system. But today, it could be centered in the bylaws and constitutions of the churches. Some churches place more value upon their bylaws than upon what is written in the Bible. For some people, it could lie in the order of worship or the style of worship. Some people place more value on having everything stay the same—the way it has always been—than upon the fact that Jesus is the way, the truth, and the life. Some people are more interested in teaching the new converts to follow the traditions of the church than to follow Jesus.

Let us move beyond all of that. Let us be people who can be filled with God's Spirit, realizing that the goal of all of our teaching is that love can come out of a pure heart, a good conscience, and a sincere faith. For that to happen we need to be filled with the grace of God.

Paul ended the letter by simply saying, "Grace be with you." And so to you, the reader, who wants Jesus to be the focus of your faith, who wants to mature beyond arguments and controversies, who wants to become a person who will pray with all peoples in all places at all times, who wants to stay away from negative attitudes that divide people, who wants to stay away from false teachings that deceive people, who wants to maintain proper relationships with people, and who wants to take a stand for Christ—there are four words for you:

"Grace be with you."

Part Two

Passing the Baton

2 Timothy

INTRODUCTION
TO SECOND TIMOTHY

Second Timothy was Paul's last writing to Timothy, and thus to the church, before his execution. Paul had been released from his house arrest in Rome (Acts 28:30, 31). That would have been expected because charges against him were vague. Just how vague they were is apparent from Paul's last hearing in Caesarea. Paul had appealed to Caesar in order to detour a Jewish plot to send him to Jerusalem, which would have probably resulted in a deathly ambush. When Festus was preparing to send Paul to Rome, King Agrippa visited him and, upon hearing about Paul's case, asked to hear Paul himself. Festus used the opportunity to help establish the charges against Paul. As he said, "It is unreasonable to send on a prisoner without specifying the charges against him" (Acts 25:13-27).

After being released from that imprisonment, Paul did some traveling and evangelizing until he was arrested in Troas and was transported back to Rome for this last imprisonment. (See page 11 above for details of this period.)

While Paul's earlier prison letters indicated that he planned to be released, this letter did not. He was not enjoying a house arrest but was in chains (2 Timothy 1:16; 2:9). He was experiencing loneliness (2 Timothy 4:9-12), and was evidently under-dressed for the kind of coldness he was experiencing in what may have been a dungeon-like atmosphere (2 Timothy 4:13).

Paul had already had a preliminary hearing, which did not go very well for him (2 Timothy 4:16). He did not expect to get out of this imprisonment alive (2 Timothy 4:6).

Before an imminent execution, Paul longed to see Timothy and visit with him again. So he wrote this letter, asking Timothy to come to him. In case Paul was executed prior to Timothy's arrival, Paul left Timothy (and thus churches today) his farewell address that encouraged Timothy to continue keeping on with faith, boldness, commitment, and godliness. He encouraged Timothy to be a model of faithful preaching and faithful practicing of the gospel of Jesus Christ. Timothy was not only to live it, but also to "lip" it. In a real sense, Paul was passing the baton in this gospel relay race to his co-worker, Timothy.

This is a crucial letter for the church today. Every generation of Christian leaders will eventually die and leave the gospel torch to a new generation of younger people. It is not enough to just leave the next generation the right content, we must also leave them with the right kind of courage. It is not enough to give to the next generation full heads but also committed hearts. We must let them know that times will be tough—tough enough that they will suffer. We must let them know that life-styles will be changing—changes that will call for purity.

The next generation cannot depend on only what the previous generation did, but they must wrestle with what the present generation will do before God.

CHAPTER TEN

Hang in There!

2 Timothy 1

From Paul to Timothy (1:1, 2)

Paul included his credentials and how he got them—but not for Timothy's sake. Timothy knew that Paul was an apostle by the will of God. However, this letter would not be only for Timothy to read; it would also be for those whom Timothy would teach—and for the on-going church of today.

An "apostle" was someone sent by a higher authority. Paul was sent by Christ Jesus and was thus His inspired representative. In nine of Paul's thirteen letters, he referred to the source of his apostleship. In this letter, he did it by stating that he was an apostle "by the will of God." Paul had a burning conviction that what he was doing was by God's direct will, not by a church council, a committee of men, or by Paul's own initiative or action.

Paul was a called apostle. And he was an apostle "according to the promise of life that is in Christ Jesus." That meant that he was sent to proclaim the promises of life, and that life is in Christ Jesus. It was Jesus who declared, "I am the way and the truth and the life. No man comes to the Father except through me" (John 14:6).

This "promise of life" goes all the way back to Genesis 3:15. But the promise is directly related to Jesus, who died on the cross for us. Jesus died that we may live. Jesus was condemned that we might be acquitted. Jesus was declared guilty that we might be declared innocent. Jesus was buried in the grave that we might be buried in baptism. Jesus rose from the grave so we can be raised to a newness of life.

Life for us is possible because God made the promise and Jesus said, "Yes." "For no matter how many promises God has made, they are 'Yes' in Christ. And so through Him the 'Amen' is spoken by us to the glory of God" (2 Corinthians 1:20). God makes the promises; Jesus says, "Yes"; and we say, "Amen."

Amen means let it be so. If we participate in this promise of life, then we must agree to receive it with the "amen." A promise becomes a reality when the receiver actually takes the promise. If Christ has been received, the promise has been transferred into reality. It is no longer a promise to us; it is a reality. Those who are in Christ do not have to wonder whether or not they will be saved—they are saved *now*. They don't wait for the promise; they are the promise with skin on.

> And this is the testimony: God has given us eternal life, and this life is in His Son. He who has the Son has life; he who does not have the Son of God does not have life" (1 John 5:11, 12).

When Paul called Timothy his "dear son," he was using a term of endearment. In no way did Paul function as a superior to Timothy just because Paul was an apostle and Timothy was not.

The greeting to Timothy, "grace, mercy and peace," was not a greeting reserved just for Timothy. Those are realities for anyone "from God the Father and Christ Jesus our Lord."

Grace refers to God's activities for our needs. *Mercy* refers to God's sensitivity to our hurts. *Peace* refers to God's mending of broken relationships. So grace is for the needy; mercy is for the hurting; and peace is for broken relationships. Those broken relationships might be feelings of inferiority, feelings of superiority, alienations from others, and feeling separated from God because of sin.

Grace, mercy, and peace are not just to be received; they are also to be shared. The church today should be the living demonstration in the community of grace—extending ministries to any needs of people in the name of Christ. No one in the community should be able to say about the church, "They just don't understand my hurts. They don't care. They are cold-hearted." The church should be known as people of reconciliation. The church should specialize in restoring to harmony the lives of people that have been destroyed by disharmony, alienation, and frustrations. Too many times, the church handles the gospel like a ball bat, beating other people down. Grace is replaced by grouchiness. Mercy is replaced by meanness. And peace is replaced with warfare. With grace, mercy, and peace, the church has a word of

124

good news, a hand of salvation, and a model of encouragement to people in the midst of an environment that is attacked by the devil constantly.

Hang in There, Timothy! (1:3-7)

In this section, there are many important words that show the heart and humility of Paul. Those words are *serve, remember you, my prayers, tears, long to see you, joy, faith, gift of God, spirit, power, love,* and *self-discipline.*

We can see in this paragraph the tremendous power of close fellowship and friendship in the Christian family. Paul and Timothy came from two different backgrounds. Paul was from the right family—pure Jews; but Timothy was from a bi-racial family. Paul had been circumcised on the eighth day. Timothy was not circumcised until he was an adult. But both had something significant in common. They had both been raised by at least one godly parent. Both had maintained some identity and functionality with their lineage. Paul mentioned this when he talked about serving God as his forefathers did (2 Timothy 1:3). Paul's chief understanding of his apostleship was service, not status. Leaders of the church today must grow to the place that they emphasize a servant's character, not a superiority complex.

Paul was not a "touch and go" minister. It was not "out of sight, out of mind" for Paul. He lived his Christian family commitments. He constantly remembered his brothers and sisters in Christ.

So he said to Timothy that he remembered Timothy in his prayers during the day and night. Paul's writings include much about prayer. He did not believe that God quit answering prayer at the end of the Old Covenant. The church started in a prayer meeting and grew as it wrapped itself around prayer in the book of Acts. Paul was a man of prayer who so needed prayer that he wrote to others to pray for him, and he let people know that he was praying for them. There was none of this, "I'll pray for you," and then forget all about doing so. Paul was a man with a filled head (apostle), busy hands (serving), and a tender heart (tears). Timothy had tears for Paul, and certainly Paul had tears for Timothy (2 Timothy 1:4). Paul was no "Lone Ranger" Christian. He loved the fellowship of God's people and so longed to see them as he longed to see Timothy. That was necessary for the fullness of joy, and it still is. One of the reasons God's people gather together on a regular basis is to increase their joy in the fellowship of brothers and sisters in Christ.

We never know how much impact the raising of our children and grandchildren will have in the next generations. Timothy had faith because his mother and grandmother modeled faith in front of him and taught him faith (2 Timothy 1:5).

Timothy was from a religiously mixed family. His father was probably an unbeliever, for he was not circumcised. But his mother was a believing Jewess who became a Christian, and evidently his grandmother had been converted to Christ as well. Timothy was a third generation Christian. He knew the Scriptures from childhood (2 Timothy 3:15). His grandfather was probably not a Christian—thus only his grandmother is mentioned.

Here are two beautiful women. They did not decide not to attend the assembly because their husbands would not go with them. They did not use that as an excuse. They did not say, "If I have to go alone, I won't go at all." They did not say, "My husband is the spiritual head of the house; and if he does not go, I will not take that practical responsibility for myself."

The grandmother, Lois, had evidently brought up her daughter, and now Eunice had been responsible for teaching the Scriptures to Timothy from his infancy. After all, someone needs to be around to teach the little ones, "Jesus loves me, this I know, for the Bible tells me so." Someone needs to be around to go with the little ones to the closing program of VBS. Someone needs to be around to hear the little ones share with excitement the Bible stories they have learned.

Timothy had not rebelled from his upbringing, and neither had Paul. But Timothy was in a very difficult ministry. He was of a different cut from Paul. Evidently, Timothy was a bit on the timid side, while Paul certainly was not.

Paul encouraged Timothy to "fan into flame the gift of God" which was in him (2 Timothy 1:6). What does this refer to? It evidently was related to the laying on of Paul's hands. We are not sure what was meant here. It may have been that God had especially empowered Timothy for the ministry through the hands of His apostle. It may be that the gift of God was in Timothy, directly from God, and Paul commissioned Timothy to use that gift by the laying on of his hands. Thus, the laying on of hands was a type of ordination. Timothy indeed had a pastoral gift. We know that Paul invited him to join the mission team and allowed him to use his gift in service.

The gift was likened to a flame that could be fanned into a higher glow. This does not necessarily mean that Timothy was losing the fire. "Fan the flame" can simply refer to stirring it up and keeping it stirred up. That is, don't let it die down. Paul elsewhere wrote that the inner man is to be renewed day by day (2 Corinthians 4:16). For that to happen calls for us to take some responsibility in that renewal. The continual brightening of the inner flame that God has given to us is related to God's own equipment for us. God does not equip us with weakness, but with power. He does not equip us with hatred, but with love. He does not equip us with self-destruction, but with self-discipline (2 Timothy 1:7).

Sometimes our environment can be so tough that we tend to hide under a bushel. Sometimes our society is so opposed to Christianity that we become somewhat afraid. But boldness, not cowardice, is a mark of Christianity. In fact, we are told that those who have been cowards on earth will not live in Heaven (Revelation 21:8).

Notice that Timothy's ministry is related both to God's action for Timothy (gift of God) and to Timothy's responsibility for reaction with that (fan into flame). There is always God's side and our side to any ministry. We must work out what God has worked in; we must stir up what God has dropped in; we must not be so busy running here and there that we lose the inner man that God has given us to guard. God has grace for us, but we must have gumption with it. God has mercy for us, but we must have management. God has peace for us, but we must have practice. God has power for us, but we must have persistence. God has love for us, and we must labor. God has the Spirit for us, and we must have service and sacrifice.

No one is to become a Christian and then just sit around with hands folded, waiting for Jesus to come back. We are to be daily in the process of being changed into His likeness (2 Corinthians 3:18). We are to be offering ourselves as living sacrifices with a transformation of the way we think and live (Romans 12:1, 2).

There was a time in the Old Testament when a prophet told a parable, using himself as the main character. He told the king that he had been given the responsibility of guarding a prisoner in battle, but then "got busy with other things, and the man

127

escaped" (1 Kings 20:39, 40; Today's English Version). Another translation says, "While your servant was busy here and there, he was gone" (New American Standard Bible). Isn't it easy for that to happen to the inner man that God has given us to guard? It is easy to get too busy; it is easy to be running to and fro. If the devil cannot make us bad, he will make us too busy to fan the flame that God has given to us.

We are gifted people. Every Christian is gifted by God (1 Corinthians 12). We must guard the gift.

Guard the Gospel (1:8-12)

Not only must we fan the gift within us, but we must guard the gospel. There are several key words that relate to that in this paragraph: *saved, holy life, do not be ashamed, suffering for the gospel, know whom I have believed, am convinced, He is able to guard, keep, pattern of sound teaching, faith, love, guard the good deposit, with the help of the Holy Spirit.*

The opposite of being timid (2 Timothy 1:7) is not being ashamed (2 Timothy 1:8). But not being ashamed could be a passive reaction. God wants a positive reaction; so attached to the words *not be ashamed* are the words *to testify.* We are to talk about what God has done in Christ and what Christ has done for us. It is a shame that we in Christianity are so divided over minor issues. It is Christ that unites us to God and to one another. But Christians have discovered certain teachings that are valuable to them; they think that no one else has seen those gems of truth and then group themselves around those minor gems of truth. Thus, denominations form. Those minor gems might be a particular understanding of the ministry of the Holy Spirit, a millennial issue, God's system of "election," the frequency of partaking of the Lord's Supper, church government, or some other. Christians then begin to judge other people's relationship to them as spiritual brothers and sisters by their perspectives on these minor issues rather than by their position in Christ. And we will spend a lot of energy marketing our opinions about many issues that have little to do with attracting the non-Christian to Jesus Christ for salvation.

Too many times, various congregations in a community are in competition with each other for members who will rally around the minor issues rather than sharing in any cooperation in the community to win people to Christ—regardless of those minor issues. No wonder the pagan world is confused today, and no wonder Jesus prayed for the Christian world to come to a place of unity (John 17).

It is the gospel that deserves our priority. That gospel is the good news that our sins can be forgiven in Christ. It was in Christ that God saved us (2 Timothy 1:9) and called us to a holy life. The holy life means a life that is set apart for God—not settled in our own selfishness.

The gospel comes out of God's grace, not out of our greatness (2 Timothy 1:9). This grace is "in Christ Jesus," not in all of our doctrinal issues that have divided Christendom so significantly and scandalously. It is this gospel—salvation in Jesus Christ—that was planned and purposed "before the beginning of time." That means that before God created humans, He wanted them to live with Him forever. Out of that intense desire for us, God designed a redemptive plan before man came in the event that man would sin against God. So God's plan announced in Genesis 3:15 was not an afterthought.

Isn't it a mark of God's great love for us that He made up His mind that He would sacrifice His Son on the cross for man even before man was formed? Any lesser God would have decided not to create man if it was going to be that costly.

It is in Christ Jesus that death is destroyed, and life and immortality are brought to light (2 Timothy 1:10). When Paul said death is destroyed, he was not saying our physical death would end; for we continue to die physically. He meant the separation from God that is caused by sin (Romans 6:23). Those who physically die outside of Christ will experience the "second death"—an eternal separation from God—when Jesus comes again (Revelation 20:14; 21:8).

Christ is not just in the destruction business (destroying death), but also the construction business (life and immortality). Life is what happens here and now. It is the forgiven life, the holy life, the saved life, the secure life, the loved life, the spirit-filled life, and the servant-life. Immortality is the transformed life beyond this earth. Then our mortal will put on the immortal. The weak will put on power, the temporary will put on the permanent (1 Corinthians 15).

Isn't it interesting that Paul, who was facing imminent physical death, spoke so confidently about the fact that Christ had destroyed death and brought life and immortality into human existence? Paul was facing death, but not defeat. He was not looking at the end of earthly life—but beyond it. He looked with hope, not despair.

One of the most characteristic attitudes of a Christian is seen when he faces death. The funeral service for a Christian should really be a celebration service. Some Christians want all songs at their funerals to be positive, celebrative, and encouraging. For the Christian, death is a promotion. For the Christian, death is more of a reunion than a separation. It is a moment of supreme joy, not deep sadness. However, the survivors will go through some grief. We do that any time we are separated from our friends and loved ones—when they go on a long journey, or away to college, or into the military service—but the grief is not despair, hopelessness, or pessimism.

Any suffering we undergo in this life is temporary. The apostle Paul spoke about suffering rather than status (2 Timothy 1:12). And yet we do everything we can to keep from suffering. Do we think that if we are suffering in any way, we are being punished? We must not cave in to the mentality of the name-it-and-claim-it fad that is spreading across Christianity. Nor must we cave in to the mentality that God will not permit any of His people to suffer. There is no teaching that God wants all of us to drive Cadillacs, wear diamond rings, have large bank accounts, or wear the most expensive clothing. Those are teachings of self-centered people, not suffering servant-saints.

If everything is supposed to be so smooth and rosy for Christians, Paul would not have been talking about death, nor would he have been inviting Timothy to visit him in prison. He would only have to "name it and claim it," and tell Timothy he would be seeing him soon back in Ephesus.

Instead, Paul gave to Timothy the torch to carry when Paul was executed. He encouraged Timothy to "keep as the pattern of sound teaching" what he has heard from Paul (2 Timothy 1:13). *Sound teaching* refers to healthy teaching. God's teaching brings health to individuals and to the body of Christ. That does not mean that one who follows His teaching will not get sick, but it does mean that there is a therapeutic value to the good news of God. It affects us more wholistically than many of us will ever know—until we get to Heaven.

Timothy was not to be flippant with the gospel—nor are we. It is a treasure to be guarded, but we are not on "guard duty" alone.

We will "guard it with the help of the Holy Spirit who lives in us" (2 Timothy 1:14). And remember that Spirit is the Spirit of power, love, and self-discipline. We must keep guarding those three characteristics; they are powerful offenses and defenses with the gospel of Jesus. We must keep them "on duty" day and night. We must not let any of those three "sentries" go to sleep. The following characteristics are also to be on duty: courage, talking about the Lord, suffering (not just status), holy living, and sound teaching.

The *pattern* that Paul referred to in verse 13 means a model or example. It is something to be copied. We are to apply it and copy it not only with our lips, but also with our lives. What Timothy heard from Paul, he was to live out as well as teach. That is the way it is to be with us.

In summary, Paul was instructing Timothy to hang in there by guarding the gospel carefully, spreading it effectively, and suffering for it faithfully.

Paul's Abandonment (1:15-18)

Not everyone will stick with us when we stand up for Christ. Many times we will find ourselves standing alone. Paul was abandoned by more people than he ever dreamed. In fact, he said "everyone in the province of Asia" had deserted him. But he was not left totally alone (2 Timothy 1:15).

The church today needs people who are like Onesiphorus (2 Timothy 1:16). He did not go along with the crowd. He came in when others walked out. He searched for Paul while others were hiding from him (2 Timothy 1:17). He stayed with Paul when others abandoned him. He held Paul up when others let him down.

The devil will always try to attack God's spokesmen—even today. He will stir people up against them—at times even the leaders of the church itself, the elders, deacons, teachers, and other influential people. A man who is determined to guard the gospel will need the Onesiphorus-type people in the church.

If you can't be a Paul or a Timothy, then be an Onesiphorus. Never mind whether you can spell it or even pronounce it—just imitate him!

CHAPTER ELEVEN

Be Strong

2 Timothy 2

Be Strong in God's Grace (2:1, 2)

It was not enough for Timothy just to fan into flame his gift for ministry (2 Timothy 1:6). He needed to be strong in the midst of an environment that was anti-godly. The strength to resist caving in to the environment would require inner commitment on Timothy's part. That is why Paul said, "Be strong in the grace." He was no doubt referring to the gift of God mentioned in 2 Timothy 1:6. For that gift is a grace-gift. No one can render services to God apart from God's equipping grace. Elsewhere, Paul referred to his ministry as a ministry that came to him "by the grace of God" (1 Corinthians 3:10). That it is God's grace that equips us for ministry is expanded in Ephesians 4:7-16. The body of Christ builds itself up as each part does its work with the grace God has given it.

An effective person cannot receive a grace-gift from God for service in the name of Christ and then just sit around waiting for that gift to do something. We must take the initiative to use that grace-gift. Peter emphasized that when he said, "Each one should use whatever gift he has received to serve others, faithfully administering God's grace in its various forms" (1 Peter 4:10). To fail to use it is to become weak in it. That is a law of life—use it or lose it. The rest of this chapter develops how Timothy was to "be strong in the grace"—the service, the ministry, the work of our Lord. The lessons are applicable to us, too.

The first way to be strong in the grace is to be sure one is not just preserving it for himself, but passing it on to others. Those who teach others will quickly affirm that through the process of teaching, they grow themselves. We will become stronger as we teach others.

But notice what Timothy was told to pass on—"the things you have heard from me." And notice to whom he was to pass it—

133

"reliable men who will also be qualified to teach others." Paul may have potential elders in mind. Remember that one of the problems in the church at Ephesus was that certain men were teaching false doctrines (1 Timothy 1:3). One of the qualifications of an elder is that he be "able to teach" (1 Timothy 3:2). It is certain that men will not reach the maturity to be able to teach without being taught. So Paul urged Timothy to teach others, and, in the process, revealed several truths for the church today.

(1) There is an apostolic succession of truth. The church is built upon the foundation of the apostles and prophets (Ephesians 2:20) and must stay on that foundation. Timothy was not to develop his own theological system. He was to pass on what the apostle had taught him. What he received from Paul, "the good deposit" (2 Timothy 1:14), he was to invest in others. That way, spiritual dividends would multiply. The church today must always be measuring its "deposit of teaching" by apostolic truth. This apostolic truth, first of all, came from Christ to Paul; then from Paul to Timothy; then from Timothy to reliable men; then from reliable men to others. What was passed on then is what we now find in the New Testament. The church today must be grounded in New Testament teaching.

(2) People must be open to be taught by others. Remember, Timothy was a younger person; it would have been easy for older men to refuse to be taught by someone whom they might have seen as a young whippersnapper. That happens many times today when older men who have been in the church a long time are closed-minded to a young preacher who comes on the scene. The reluctance to be taught by others could be one reason many churches are in trouble today when it comes to understanding and applying the Word. When there is a breakdown in any one generation, it is likely that the breakdown will be passed on to other generations.

(3) Those who are taught must teach others. No Christian leader has the right to keep understandings to himself as a power-play. The world teaches that the more you know, the more power you wield. But the Christian system is, the more you know, the more you must share.

(4) Those who teach must equip others to teach. We must be recruiting new teachers continuously by equipping them. One of the reasons many churches are in trouble today is because they will permit any volunteer to teach. Many churches have no idea

what is being taught in their church schools, youth groups, men's meetings, women's societies, or other groups/classes. Few churches have a program of teaching people for the purpose of qualifying them to teach others, who in turn will teach others to teach. Few members come to the Sunday school or other training meetings for the purpose of seeing themselves as becoming equipped as teachers of others.

Isn't it interesting that most of us attend various schools with the intention of graduating and using the information we gained outside the school? Who goes to kindergarten expecting to stay there? Who goes to high school expecting not to graduate? Yet isn't it true that many go to the Sunday school for thiry or forty years and never intend to graduate to being a teacher of others?

Christian leaders are not just to pass on content, however. There are several attitudes, activities, reactions, and characteristics, that must be passed on as well. And these are as much a part of apostolic truth as the content. The rest of this chapter picks up many of those aspects, such as enduring hardship, remaining faithful, having integrity, being a hard worker, remembering Jesus Christ, refraining from quarreling, being an approved workman, being noble, fleeing evil desires, pursuing righteousness, faith, love, and peace, being kind, and not being resentful.

The rest of this chapter not only shows various characteristics that need to be passed on to become a part of the characters of Christian leaders, but also shows how a Christian leader is to remain "strong in the grace that is in Christ Jesus."

Paul packaged how to be strong in illustrations that any culture can understand—soldier, athlete, farmer, workman, vessel, and servant. In the middle of all that, he reminded Timothy of our commander in chief, the Lord Jesus Christ (2 Timothy 2:7-13).

The Soldier (2:3, 4)

Many military words were used in the first-century language to describe the Christian life. Those included words like *soldier, army, armor, shield, sword, helmet, breastplate, guard, be on the alert,* and *fight the good fight.* Using military metaphors was a popular way to communicate aspects of Christianity.

Having faith in Christ is to believe in a new commander in chief. Repentance is a decision to become a deserter to Satan—to change sides. Baptism is the oath-taking ceremony that transfers one from one kingdom to another. Prayer is keeping contact with the command post. Worship and education are the spiritual supply depots for the battle in the front lines.

The military metaphor zeroes in on several essentials of the Christian life: soldiering, suffering, serving, separation, and pleasing. The most basic concept is *soldiering* —a commitment to get into the battle. Boot camp is for the purpose of preparation for the front-line battles. But some Christians remain in boot camp; some stay in the barracks; some act as if they are A.W.O.L. (away without official leave); some seem to have taken early retirement; some have deserted (Paul mentioned some of those in 2 Timothy 1:15).

There is indeed a battle going on, and the Christian must be involved in that battle. We are not fighting against flesh and blood, but principalities and powers in Heavenly places (Ephesians 6:12). Christians must be strong in the Lord and put on the full armor of God (Ephesians 6:10, 11).

Suffering is a part of soldiering. A soldier changes his life-style, habits, dress, conduct, and place of living in order to serve his commander. A soldier is on twenty-four-hour notice. He can be transferred quickly to another location. Not many enter into soldiering with a pay increase. Soldiers don't normally drive along the front lines in air-conditioned limousines. Hair spray and toothpaste are often considered luxuries. They carry heavy loads, spend long days with little sleep; and when they do sleep, they are often in cold, wet situations. They watch their friends get wounded and killed; they themselves get shot at and sometimes wounded. They get very little praise, for they are simply doing their duty.

Soldiers are known for *service*. In fact, one of the terms used for military life is "the service." The Christian life is a life of service, not of status. It is being on the front lines with the heavy loads, the long days, and the lonely nights. We can get shot at and wounded, but we continue; we are commissioned to take every thought captive and to obey Christ (2 Corinthians 10:5).

Soldiering involves *separation*. The soldier does not "get involved in civilian affairs" (2 Timothy 2:4). That does not mean he is not to be a good citizen in a community, but it does mean that he lives, first of all, for carrying out the responsibilities of his command post.

Paul meant that the Christian is not to get tangled up in his former life-style. He is to break with his past. He has on a new uniform; he marches under a new flag; he is to live like a soldier of Christ, not like someone who has not enlisted in God's army.

During the early centuries of Christianity, the Latin word for being a civilian was *pagani*. A *pagani* was not involved in the military in any way. It was that Latin word that was carried over into Christian talk to refer to someone who had not joined God's army. That non-Christian was referred to as a pagan. Our word *pagan* comes from that "civilian-military" terminology; the civilian in this metaphor is the non-Christian. So when Paul talked about Timothy's being a soldier who did not get involved in civilian affairs, he was referring to a Christian's not getting involved in pagan affairs. He is to make the break. Learn to say no. Learn to flee. Learn to run. Live the holy life to which God has called us (2 Timothy 1:9).

Some of the "civilian affairs" are mentioned later on in this chapter. They include evil desires of youth, foolish and stupid arguments, quarrels, and being resentful. In order to avoid getting involved in those kind of pagan affairs, a person must sharpen his senses for the purpose of escaping from "the trap of the devil" (2 Timothy 2:26).

A soldier is also interested in *pleasing* his commanding officer. The Christian's commander in chief is Jesus. Every Christian should grow in his commitment to the place that his primary purpose is to please Jesus in everything. Paul elsewhere wrote that we are to "make it our goal to please him" (2 Corinthians 5:9). Promotions come by pleasing the commanding officer. There will be rewards in Heaven for those whose chief ambition was to please Jesus. We don't please Him for the purpose of getting rewards. We please Him out of respect and love to Him.

One of the first ways we can please our commanding officer is by being willing to obey. We don't argue or question the orders. We don't refuse to do them unless the whole battle plan is spelled out. We don't demand explanations. We trust our commanding officer so much that when He says, "Jump," our only question is, "How high?"

The Athlete (2:5)

There are several essential aspects of athletics that directly relate to the Christian life: An athlete stays in shape. An athlete practices. An athlete competes. An athlete sticks to the rules. An athlete uses self-discipline.

The Christian is to remain *in shape*. That is the reason Paul began this chapter encouraging Timothy to be strong. As an athlete stays in shape by what he does and by what he stays away from, so does the Christian. No athlete stays in shape or becomes strong without some pain. No pain—no gain. An athlete cannot stay in shape without some stretching; Christians need to be willing to stretch their spiritual muscles. We must be willing to grow daily into the likeness of Christ.

The Christian must *practice*. Some athletes practice for hours and hours every day. The Christian must know that he is not just called to a position, but also to a practice. And that practice must be exercised daily. It is the practice of godliness. It is the practice of Christlikeness. It is the practice of holding the tongue. It is the practice of thinking holy thoughts. It is the practice of staying away from unholy situations. It is the practice of controlling desires.

An athlete *competes*, and the Christian is also to be in the competitive arena. But Christians are not to compete with other Christians; that is where we have got off base many times. It is easy for Christians to compare themselves with other Christians, but one who does that is without understanding. God has gifted us differently from the competitive arena. We are to compete against the devil and his forces. If a Christian can understand this and accept this, then he will not be jealous of another Christian because of his activity. He will not be envious of another Christian because of his position. Christians are to compete against our opponent—the devil—as a team. We are to do everything we can to help our other team members. It is the team that is to win, not just individual Christians.

As an athlete *sticks to the rules* (or is disqualified), even so Christians are to stick to God's rules lest they be disqualified. Paul elsewhere mentioned that he had to keep his body in shape daily lest he become disqualified (1 Corinthians 9:27). Christians are to stick to the rules in their relationship with God; their relationship to the church, their relationship to the world, and their relationship to others.

What are those rules? Read through Ephesians 4 and 5 for a start. If you don't want that heavy of an assignment, slip down and read verses 22-25 here in this chapter.

Christians must be *self-disciplined*. An athlete who loses his self-discipline will soon get out of shape, quit practicing, begin to fear competition, and try to bend the rules. And a Christian who does not manifest self-discipline will eventually do the same. Christians must not live by "maybe," but rather let their yes be yes and their no be no. They must know what they have said yes to and what it is they are committed to saying no to. They must determine to stick with the life and stand against what the world says. A good athlete does not pay attention to what other people are thinking, saying, or doing; he has his goal in mind and is committed to reaching it. One of the main differences between those athletes who go to the Olympics and those who don't is this matter of self-discipline.

One of the things that hampers self-discipline more than anything else is pride. Too many athletes think they don't have to exercise self-discipline because of their talent—they are good enough already. Yet they are the ones who end up watching the Olympics on television instead of participating in them.

The Farmer (2:6)

There are several aspects of a farmer's life that are essential to the Christian life as well, like faith, hard work, patience, and participation.

It takes a lot of *faith* for a farmer to farm. He puts his finest seed in the ground. In fact, he will put his last remaining seed into the ground; he does not keep back his seed for a seed savings-account. He has faith and invests it all. The farmer also has faith in God, who brings the rain and sunshine. A farmer knows that he is a failure without the partnership of God. Although he plants the seed, what happens beyond that is largely out of his control.

The Christian worker is to do the same. We are to invest our teaching, our character, our examples, our fellowship, and our discipline into the lives of others. But we are to do it in partnership with God, who can bring the spiritual sunshine and water that will bring growth.

The farmer is a *hard worker.* He prepares the soil, plants the seed, cultivates the field, repairs the machinery, and keeps abreast of new methods. He does not just pray for a harvest; he works for it.

There is to be a real balance between prayer and work in the Christian life. Jesus prayed much, but He also worked hard. Jesus said we were to pray for laborers for the harvest. Why didn't He just tell us to pray for the harvest? Because there is a relationship between praying and perspiring. No church grows today without hard work.

The farmer is also *patient*. He must wait for the rain and the sun. He must wait for the seed to germinate. He must wait for the plant to break through the soil. He must wait for maturity. The Christian worker must also be willing to wait. We cannot plant the seed of Christ in another, and then pull that person up by the roots, so to speak, to see why he is not growing. Too much of that will kill the fruit. Impatience has led some Christians to criticize, badmouth the setbacks, and discourage others.

A farmer also *participates* in his crops. Few farmers starve to death. They don't grow crops just to feed others. They also intend to feed themselves. The Christian worker must also participate in what he is planting. We must not plant God's Word for someone else to eat, while we ourselves do not eat of God's Word, prayer, worship, meditation, and holy living.

There is another application to what Paul said about the farmer's receiving a share of the crops that every leader of the church must be sensitive to. That is, that churches must provide materially for their preachers. Paul said, "If we have sown spiritual seed among you, is it too much if we reap a material harvest from you?" (1 Corinthians 9:11). In that passage, Paul used the metaphor of the farmer to talk about the church's caring for its preachers (1 Corinthians 9:10).

It is a shame to see how some church leaders will refuse to share benefits with their preachers—an action that would cause them great consternation if their employers did the same to them! In fact, they would form unions and walk out. Preaching is hard work. The Christian life is hard work. If it weren't so hard, everybody would be in it.

Our Commander in Chief (2:7-13)

Jesus Christ is the chief model of a good soldier, a good athlete, and hard-working farmer. One can trace His life in Matthew, Mark, Luke, and John and spot the times that His characteristics reflected those of a soldier, an athlete, and a farmer.

He is the one who can give insight about how to be a soldier, an athlete, and farmer (2 Timothy 2:7). And He is the commander in chief that all of the Christian troops should remember (2 Timothy 2:8). He is the commander in chief who was mortally wounded but would not remain dead. That is a great commander to follow!

140

He suffered and died for the church; that is the reason Paul said that everything he did he did for the sake of the elect.

An athlete does not perform only for himself but also for the team. A soldier does not do it for himself only, but also for his country and fellow soldiers. A farmer does not farm just for himself but also to feed others. And no Christian is to live just for himself—but for others, the elect. We are to invest our lives so that others may also have the salvation that is in Christ Jesus. Remember, we pray, "*Our* Father," not "*My* Father." And we also pray, "Give *us our* daily bread."

To the degree that the church forgets Jesus and focuses in on other people or other issues, we will be in the wrong battle, compete against the rules, and sow the wrong seeds. Individual Christians and churches do that as they settle in on minor issues and emphasize those rather than Jesus Christ.

Remembering Jesus is stated in some positive and some negative expressions. The positives are dying with Him and enduring with Him.

1. *Dying with Him* (2 Timothy 2:11) refers to our giving up our former lives and being buried in baptism (Romans 6). When that happens, we will live with Him. We will rise to walk in a newness of life—His kind of living. The soldier must be literally willing to die. The athlete must be willing to die to what many others are doing (the distractions). The seed that the farmer plants dies in order to produce life.

2. *To endure with Him* here is to suffer for His cause. If we do, we will reign with Him forever (2 Timothy 2:12). It is that hope that keeps us going—even to the point of death (see above).

The negatives are expressed in 2 Timothy 2:12 and 13. They are disowning Him and being faithless.

1. *We must not disown Him,* or He will disown us (2 Timothy 2:12). The soldier must trust his commanding officer. The athlete must trust his coach. The farmer must trust the seed and God who provides the weather.

2. *We must not be faithless* (2 Timothy 2:13). If we are faithless to Him, He will not go along with us. He will remain faithful, to himself. If we are faithless to the battle, He will remain faithful to it. If we are faithless to the team, He will be faithful to it. If we are faithless to sowing the seed, He will be faithful to it.

"If we are faithless, He will remain faithful" (2 Timothy 2:13). This does not mean that He will approve our faithlessness. It does

141

not mean He will be faithful to *us* if we are faithless to Him. He has just finished saying that if we disown Him, He will disown us. Instead, it means that Christ will remain faithful to His purpose, to His character, and to His goal regardless of what we do. The commander in chief will not become a deserter when some of his troops leave. The coach will not give up on the team because one athlete is no longer committed. God is in the business of changing us; we will not change Him.

All of us need a rallying point from time to time. For the Christian that point is always, "Remember Jesus Christ" (2 Timothy 2:8). That is the battle cry for the soldier. It is like the slogan, "Remember Pearl Harbor," in that it is our motivation for action. It would be like saying to the athlete, "Remember the team." It would be like saying to the farmer, "Remember the joys of the harvest." It is a word of encouragement in the midst of discouragement. It is a word of motivation in the midst of apathy. It is the order of the day for the soldier, the cheerleader's chant for the athlete, and the word of hope for the farmer.

There are some paradoxes in this section: dying is the way to live, enduring is the way to reign. But if we doubt it, just "remember Jesus Christ." He proved it.

The Approved Workman (2:14-19)

There are several essentials for being an approved workman: he doesn't quarrel, he is competent, he avoids majoring in minors, he doesn't wander from the main task, and he is committed to personal moral values.

Workmen who are always quarreling will not provide quality work (2 Timothy 2:14). And so it is with Christians in the church. Good workmen are to be competent, and so are Christians. The one who deals with the Word is to be one who "correctly handles the word of truth" (2 Timothy 2:15). The word translated "correctly handles" literally means to cut straight. Don't be taking side detours with the Word. Don't be cutting corners. Don't be dodging the important issues.

The idea of cutting straight comes from the concept of plowing a field. A farmer in that day would set his eyes on a distant goal and use that as a guiding point. As long as he kept his eyes on the goal, he could cut a straight furrow across the field.

Our goal for teaching is to enable people to be like Christ, not for them to think we are smart and creative. We are not to read into the Word what is not there. We are to keep it in context, compare it with other Scriptures, and stay with the intention of the writers. We are not only to know what it says, but also what it means. We are to apply it to our lives today.

If our goal is to have people focus on our great knowledge and teaching ability, then we have not handled the Word correctly. If our goal is to cause people to belong to "our" group, then we have not handled the Word correctly. If our goal is to criticize everyone else, then we have not handled the Word correctly.

If our teaching leads to godless chatter, then we have not handled the Word correctly. If our teaching leads men astray, then we have not handled the Word correctly (2 Timothy 2:18). If our teaching leads to wickedness, then we have not handled the Word correctly (2 Timothy 2:19).

We are not to be quarreling about words (2 Timothy 2:14), chattering about ungodly things (2 Timothy 2:16), wandering from the truth (2 Timothy 2:18), challenging mainline doctrines about Jesus (2 Timothy 2:18), destroying people's faith (2 Timothy 2:18), causing people to doubt their salvation (2 Timothy 2:18), being involved in wickedness (2 Timothy 2:19), being loose in morals (2 Timothy 2:20, 21), and failing to flee evil desires (2 Timothy 2:22).

There are two kinds of workmen—one who is approved and one who is ashamed (2 Timothy 2:15). The ashamed workman is one whose work is not acceptable, regardless of how much energy he puts into it. The building he has built (people's lives) will come crumbling down. The approved workman will build upon God's solid foundation (2 Timothy 2:19), while refraining from quarreling, majoring in minors, and wandering from the truth. At the same time, he will be competent in how he handles the Word and in how he lives in the world. He will handle the Word by cutting it straight. He will live in the world by walking away from and/or fighting against wickedness.

The Vessel (2:20, 21)

A Christian is a vessel of lasting quantity and quality. He is referred to as a vessel of gold and silver, not of wood and clay. The gold and silver are long lasting. The wood and clay are not. The difference is whether or not a person cleanses himself from what is ignoble. The useful vessel is holy—that is, he sets himself apart for God's life-style and God's priorities. Consequently, he is useful to the Master and is ready for any kind of good work (2 Timothy 2:21).

This small paragraph in this passage is sandwiched between two verses that are essential to an understanding of clean vessels. One verse gives the command to "turn away from wickedness" (2 Timothy 2:19). The other verse commands, "Flee the evil desires of youth" (2 Timothy 2:22). Both of those verses make clear man's responsibility for being clean. God cleanses us in Jesus Christ, but we have a responsibility for keeping ourselves useful and clean. It is not all God's work, and it is not all our work. It is a partnership.

This type of partnership and cooperation is seen in the examples previously given. There is a team relationship between the commanding officer and the trooper. There is a team relationship between an athlete and the others on the team. There is a partnership between the farmer and the elements (and God). The person who is going to be fit for God's use must remember Jesus Christ (2 Timothy 2:8) and be committed to keeping himself clean (2 Timothy 2:20, 21).

The Servant (2:22-26)

Being strong in the grace of the Lord (2 Timothy 2:1) calls for the servant to engage in several positive, penetrating, and powerful activities and attitudes. These include fleeing, pursuing, being kind, and gently instructing.

The Christian servant must *flee* the evil desires of youth (2 Timothy 2:22). These involve desires of arrogance, of independence, of impatience, of self-love, of sensuality, of temper-tantrums, and other immature desires. But it is not enough to flee; the servant must actively *pursue*. That word refers to using energy in chasing something until one has caught it. Christian service must chase down the following until they are acquired:

1. Righteousness—a right relationship with God, self and others.
2. Faith—a trust in God.
3. Love—an outgoing commitment for someone else's well-being.
4. Peace—the absence of alienation and disharmony.

This pursuing must be done *with* others who are God's—not against them.

Some Christians have disengaged from the church in order to become private "Lone Ranger" Christians. Some feel they can pursue the Christian walk in the privacy of their living rooms. To disengage from the church is to disengage from God's family and the means for gaining maturity.

The Lord's servant must manifest *kindness* to everyone, instead of quarreling to win individual battles. He must be able to teach and not be resentful of times when he has been misunderstood, hurt, ignored, and spoken against. If he is kind, not resentful, and able to teach—then it will all be wrapped up in instruction that is gentle in the hope that God will nurture the seed that was planted and bring others to a change of mind. That calls for the patience of a farmer; that calls for a soldier who will fight according to the commander's strategies. That calls for an athlete who will run the race according to God's rules.

Only then have we competed well against the devil. Only then will we have won the battle against his tricks. Only then will we have planted a seed that he will not be able to uproot and destroy. And we will have no reason to be ashamed.

Then he will be able to be strong in the grace that is in Christ Jesus!

We can chase people away; and when we do, we will chase them toward the devil, who has a trap ready for them. We chase people away when we hang onto our evil desires, do not manifest right personal relationships, hate instead of love, hold bitterness against people (not peace), initiate an involvement in quarrels and arguments, are rude instead of being kind, dictate instead of teach, are resentful instead of being forgiving, and instruct harshly instead of being gentle.

Some people love the truth, but they cannot stand the attitudes of the Christians that surround them. Thus, they move from the truth of God to the trap of the devil. Without knowing it, without intending for it to happen, they become captive to do the devil's will.

God's servants must be rescuers, actively involved in the rescue team to release Satan's P.O.W.s (prisoners of war). Want to be on God's rescue team? Then open yourself up to "be strong in the grace that is in Christ Jesus." What does it mean to be strong? Read this chapter again.

CHAPTER TWELVE

Live a Godly Life

2 Timothy 3

Sensuality (3:1-5)

This chapter is directly connected with the preceding chapter by the first word, *but,* which introduces a contrast. Paul had finished the last chapter on an optimistic note—that God would grant that some would come to repentance and escape from the trap of the devil.

However, lest Timothy believe that would happen to everyone, Paul brought to Timothy the flip side of life. That is summarized in the sentence, "There will be terrible times in the last days."

The Greek word translated "terrible" emphasizes something that is hard. Some Greeks used the word to describe wild animals or the raging sea. It referred to a situation that was indeed difficult to tame and difficult to escape without some pain and discomfort.

And it will happen in the "last days." The last days does not describe a period of time ahead of us that will begin just before the second coming. We must not use earth's calendar to describe the "last days," but rather Heaven's chronology. Biblically speaking, *the last days* refers to the "last age" prior to the second coming. That is the Christian age in which we are now living.

The writer of Hebrews identified the "last days" as beginning with the first coming of Jesus Christ (Hebrews 1:1, 2). On the day of Pentecost, Peter made it clear that the happenings of that day were the evidences that the "last days" had begun (Acts 2:16-21).

So the kinds of life-style Paul was describing to Timothy in the "last days" is not a life-style that is only in our future, but was also in Timothy's environment and will be in every environment until Jesus Christ comes again.

Those times will be "terrible," whether we live in mansions or shacks, whether we have no money or have millions, whether we have feast or famine, whether we are healthy or diseased. The terribleness has to do with our morals, not our materials. The way people live with one another makes life either terrible or terrific.

The descriptions of the kind of people that make life terrible could be summed up in one word—*selfish*. These are people who do not recognize the essentiality of being connected with other people with interdependence upon them and gratefulness for them. It is indeed interesting that, having lived 2,000 years with the advances of psychology, sociology, and technology, we continue to be a very disconnected people. We can be connected with people around the world via the electronic media, but not be connected with people in our own homes. We can reach out to people in other parts of the globe via the telephone, but fail to touch the people in our neighborhood with care, compassion, and love.

Life is terrific when we live within Jesus' two greatest commandments—love God and love people as ourselves (Matthew 22:37-40). But life is terrible when we neglect God and fail to see the potential in other people; when we keep God and other people at a distance; when we do not live in harmony with other people; when we do not acknowledge the necessary dependence upon God and interdependence upon one another; in short, when we do not submit to God and to the "one anothers" in the Bible. The people described in this paragraph do not have the relational skills to make life terrific.

Let's consider how Paul described the breakdown.

Relationship to Self

The relationship to self is described in five ways: "lovers of themselves, lovers of money, boastful, proud, abusive" (2 Timothy 3:2). All of these are interrelated. A person who is a lover of himself and not of others will be a lover of money, because he cannot use his money cheerfully for the benefit of others. He sees money only as a means to benefit himself. Money is used to enhance love toward himself. He accumulates more things because he believes he deserves more things. Such a person becomes boastful and proud. He will inwardly think that he is better than others (proud), and outwardly show it by being abusive.

This person lives in opposition to God's original creation. God created man to love God, self, and others and to dominate over things. But sin entered into the world, and man turned God's intention around—he began to love things and dominate over others, including trying to control God. That act of rebellion and domination is seen in the next relational dimension.

Relationship With Family

The relationship with one's family was summed up when Paul wrote "disobedient to parents" (2 Timothy 3:2). This is the natural outgrowth when someone loves self and thinks he is better than even his parents.

The next two characteristics also probably relate to a person's family life—"ungrateful" and "unholy." That is, ungrateful to his parents and without commitment to the family. The words *holy* and *unholy* were sometimes used in classical Greek to refer to a person's commitment to his family. When two were committed to each other, they were "holy." When they were committed to the marriage, they were "holy." When the parents were committed to their children and children to their parents, they were "holy." (See 1 Corinthians 7:12-14.)

The breakdown in family relationships begins with a false evaluation of God and self.

Relationship With Others

The next nine characteristics (2 Timothy 3:3, 4) refer to a person's relationship both in the family and beyond the family. A person who is not in love with God but is in love with himself will manifest the following characteristics:

1. He does not have a healthy concern for others ("without love").
2. He carries grudges ("unforgiving"). He is the type who says, "I don't get mad; I just get even."
3. He uses his tongue to ruin the reputation of others ("slanderous").
4. He uses no self-restraint in getting ahead, regardless of the people he hurts along the way ("without self-control").
5. He is "brutal."
6. He has no concern for doing things for the benefit of others ("not lovers of the good").
7. He is deceitful in his relationships ("treacherous").
8. He is reckless in both thought and words ("rash").
9. He looks at others only through a puffed up image of himself ("conceited").

Relationship With Things

A selfish person's relationship with things is summed up in the last half of 2 Timothy 3:4, "lovers of pleasure." Consequently, things are accumulated for pleasure. He may also accumulate people for pleasure. He lives for the now, not the future. He lives for things, not truth. He lives for materials, not the Master. He wants entertainment, not enlightenment. He is more interested in fun than faithfulness.

Relationship With God

Lovers of self and pleasure are not "lovers of God." Isn't it interesting that Jesus' two greatest commandments bracket this set of characteristics? Jesus said that the greatest commandments were to love God and to love others (Matthew 22:34-40). Jesus made it clear that having those two commandments down pat would be the basis upon which all other commandments are fulfilled. When those two commandments are violated, the doors are open for all kinds of inhuman attitudes and actions.

Paul started the listing with a person's failure to love others (2 Timothy 3:2) and concluded with a person's failure to love God (2 Timothy 3:4). Loving God and loving others are related. You have probably seen this relationship illustrated with a picture of a triangle. God is at the top and a person is at each base angle. The closer those two people at the bottom of the triangle get to God at the top, the closer they get to each other. That is an eternal spiritual law of God. A person will not move toward getting closer to God or others if he centers on self-love only.

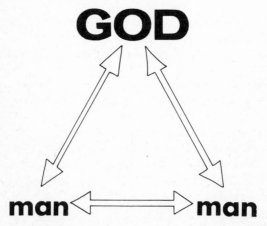

Relationship to Religion

The person described above is not necessarily a person outside the religious organization. He may be squarely in the middle of the church. He may be a leader. He may say the right words, attend the right meetings, and give the right amount of money. But he is doing it all for the benefits to himself. He is a counterfeit Christian. He is following a "form of godliness but denying its power" (2 Timothy 3:5).

The power of godliness is the presence of the Holy Spirit, that moves us from self-centeredness to God-centeredness, which leads to concern for others. A person cannot be filled with the power of the Holy Spirit and continue to live in a self-centered way. However, it is possible to have the "show" of Christianity without Christ's Spirit. Jesus spoke of hypocrites, who on the outside were polished, but on the inside were polluted. They were alive on the outside, but dead on the inside.

Paul had a very tough commandment for Timothy in relationship to these people: "Have nothing to do with them" (2 Timothy 3:5). Paul was not suggesting that Timothy have nothing to do with people who were outside of Christianity and had the above characteristics—that would be foolish. The only way we can introduce people to the Christ is by involvement with people. Being salt, light, and leaven emphasizes being involved with people.

However, Christians should have nothing to do with people inside the church who manifest the above characteristics. To do so affirms that such an attitude and actions are acceptable. To do so is to become vulnerable to adopting the same selfish tactics.

The Spread of Sensuality (3:6-9)

Ungodly characteristics are not just taught, but are also caught in interpersonal relationships. Paul made it clear that people with ungodly characteristics in the church do not stay to themselves. They want to spread their ungodliness by attaching people to themselves. In fact, the more people they can attach to themselves, the more their pride, arrogance, and love for themselves is elevated. Such people will feed upon those who have an inferiority complex or special human needs. As these needy people rally around the conceited, they fuel the puffed-up images of the arrogant.

These ungodly people spread sensuality in several ways: they "worm their way into homes" and "gain control" over people (2

Timothy 3:6), they "oppose the truth," have "depraved minds," and are outside "the faith" (2 Timothy 3:8). Their success is very temporary (2 Timothy 3:9). The kinds of people they go after are described in various ways: "weak-willed," guilt-ridden ("loaded down with sins"), easily persuaded ("swayed by all kinds of evil desires"), unstable in doctrine ("always learning but never able to acknowledge the truth"). These people are especially vulnerable to the conceited vultures.

The ungodly ones are deceitful; they don't let people know what they are really after; they have hidden agendas. What they really want is a person's purse or property and priorities. This same type of thing is prevalent today through the mass media. Some of the electronic evangelists worm their way into people's homes via the television and radio. They play upon people's feelings of guilt, inferiority, and weakness.

In the first century, the main target was "weak-willed women." This was probably referring to widows (1 Timothy 5). They are still the targets today of many religious con-artists. This verse does not at all mean that all women are weak-willed. It is simply describing women who are very vulnerable to the power play of others—women who need attention because they are lonely. Today, this could describe many males and females.

One of the main problems of these people who are easily swayed is that they are not firmly settled in their doctrine (2 Timothy 3:7). The church must accept part of the blame for that. A church that does not take seriously the necessity for equipping its members can expect such a result. Leaders in the church are to equip their members to do a work of ministry so they will not be tossed to and fro by every wind of doctrine that comes along (Ephesians 4:11-15).

The fact that these religious con-artists are deceptive is seen by comparing them to Jannes and Jambres (2 Timothy 3:8). These were two magicians in Pharaoh's court who opposed Moses and his mission to free the Israelites. They practiced the art of deceptive magic to lure people to them. They were professional tricksters who preyed upon the emotions and the desires for the sensational.

Why bring up Moses in this discussion? Because Moses was the leader of the Old Covenant; he brought the nation of Israel out of the slavery under Pharaoh. Moses brought God's truth to the people.

The New Testament counterpart is Christ. He leads us out of the slavery of the Pharaohs of today. Christ has set us free (Galatians 5:1). And Christ shared with us God's truth. The truth of Christ was shared with Paul, and Paul shared that truth with Timothy. Today, every genuine Christian leader must share the truth of Christ and not bring deceptive teaching or behavior for the purpose of gaining a following.

It is moral shame for leaders to use sensational methods in the name of religion to steal a person's Social Security checks, one's estate, or a person's property with the magic art of persuasive speech. Such people may go a long way for a short period of time, but really "they will not get vary far." They will eventually be exposed in this life and when Jesus comes again. "Their folly will be clear to everyone" (2 Timothy 3:9).

How do we fight against that kind of deception? We do so by knowing the apostles' teaching and methods and by determining ourselves to live a godly life. That was Paul's charge to Timothy.

Live the Godly Life (3:10-17)

The Right Model (10-13)

Instead of following the model of the religious con-artists, we ought to follow the model of the apostles. Paul gave that charge to Timothy, which included the following:

1. Apostolic teaching of the truth. Know what it is; don't chase every fad.
2. Apostolic moral conduct (way of life).
3. Apostolic aim in life (purpose). This refers to pleasing God as one's chief ambition (2 Corinthians 5:9).
4. Apostolic fidelity to Christ (faith).
5. Apostolic tolerance with people (patience). They are not trying to capture them.
6. Apostolic concern for the well-being of others (love). They are not overcome with the love of self.
7. Apostolic steadfastness with situations and events (endurance). They are not trying to twist things to go their selfish way.
8. Apostolic openness to being persecuted and to suffering. They are not out to take advantage of others.

The above characteristics describe a person who cares about others and about God.

The Right Teaching (14, 15)

Some people are embarrassed by living the Christian life as taught by their parents and preachers. But Paul made it clear that Timothy was to continue in what he had learned because he knew who taught him. Paul was probably referring to Timothy's mother and grandmother who taught him. Then, of course, he was also referring to himself as Timothy's teacher.

Don't be chasing after flashy teachers while ignoring those who have been close to us and influenced us. They may not be sensational, but they are sincere. They are not flashy, but they are faithful. They are not well-known, but they are well deserving of God's honor and our respect.

The Right Text (16, 17)

Teaching from others must square with the teaching from the text. Timothy's teaching from infancy was the teaching of the holy Scriptures.

We must realize that writings outside the Scripture are not to be our final guides for living. Some works claim to correct errors in the Bible; some claim to be additional inspiration to the Bible. Don't believe any of that. When Paul said, "All Scripture is God-breathed," he was referring to the Old Testament and his writing. He was writing as an "apostle" of Jesus Christ. That meant he was inspired by Christ to write what he did. What Timothy heard from Paul had now been put into writing and was inspired by Jesus. That is why Paul said to follow it. Peter certainly understood that Paul's letters were Scripture (2 Peter 3:15, 16).

To say that Scripture is God-breathed means that it did not come from a human source. God inspired the Bible. Its origin is from God, but its purpose is for man—"useful for teaching, rebuking, correcting and training in righteousness." Its goal is that man will be "thoroughly equipped for *every* good work." The Bible does not equip us to understand science; it does not equip us to know the technical details of our vocation, but it does equip us to do every good work by teaching the principles, the morals, the values, and the interpersonal relationships that will turn our activity into good work.

The Bible was written to train us in righteousness. Righteousness refers to expressing a proper relationship with God, self, the world, and others. Only when we have and demonstrate a right relationship with God in a wholistic way are we open for a right service for the benefit of others.

Notice that Scripture is not to be studied only so that we can have full heads. We are not to study Scriptures so that we can know more than others—in order to elevate ourselves above others. We are to study the Bible so that we can serve better and relate to others with an understanding of the mind-set and character of God. Those who know the Bible but cannot relate to others have missed a significant function of the Word of God.

If we really want to see the purpose, the benefits, and the application of the Word of God, we need to walk in the shoes of Jesus. He was the Word of God in flesh (John 1:1). How He looked at people, how He treated people, how He served people, how He looked at God, how He treated God, and how He served God are the model of what it means to be thoroughly equipped for every good work, trained in righteousness.

Some people know more about Greek than about Christ. Some know more about archaeology than *agape*. Some know more about Hebrew than humility. Some know more about memorizing Scripture than about the Master's work. Some know more about the culture of the first century than about compassion in the twentieth century.

Jesus knew more about all of the above than all human beings put together. But none of that got in His way. The woman at the well did not know that Jesus was a great scholar, but by His understanding, His compassion, and His willingness to identify with the untouchable, she realized He was the Messiah. Jesus calls us to follow His way, with His heart, filled with His Spirit, for the purpose of reconciling mankind to God. We will do it by being humble servants.

CHAPTER THIRTEEN

Preach the Word

2 Timothy 4

The Charge (4:1-5)

Paul was in prison, but he was not alone. He was "in the presence of God" (2 Timothy 4:1). That is a reminder that we are always in God's presence. There is no such thing as a "Lone Ranger" Christian—one who is accountable to no one. Even the Lone Ranger needed Tonto. The idea that no one will ever know, and thus we can follow our own feelings, does not wash with God.

We are in His presence now, and we will be in His judgment hall later—"who will judge the living and the dead." Christians will not be judged for whether or not they will be saved. Christians are saved in Christ. In Christ, there is no condemnation (Romans 8:1), but non-Christians will be declared condemned. Not the salvation, but the service of Christians will be evaluated. In view of the approaching Judgment, the charge is to "preach the Word."

The word *preach* in the Greek has to do with communicating for the purpose of a response. It is primarily (although not exclusively) referring to preaching to the non-Christian; it is an evangelistic thrust. To "preach the Word" is to preach Christ, for He is God's Word in flesh (John 1:1, 14). Some preachers spend their whole time preaching their pet doctrines, theories, outlines, and systematic theologies. Some can be full of content and empty of Christ.

It was Christ who died for us; it was Christ who was raised; it is Christ who is going to appear again. It is Christ who saves us and unites us. The doctrine that we teach ought to help us understand Christ, apply Christ, and live Christ. Another way to say "preach the Word" is to say "proclaim Christ." Some people have so zeroed in on "the Word" as the written Word—the syntax and the grammar—that they specialize in the Greek, Hebrew, and historical situations. They do a terrific job of communicating all the nuances of the written Word, but at the same time, Jesus Christ gets lost among the details. This is not to say that we should bypass the written Word. It is God's inspired message for the purpose of bringing us to Christ, understanding Christ, and living Christ. But to be so caught up in the written words on paper that we miss the Living Word is to fall into the trap of Judaism. We must allow the written Word to lead us to Christ and mature us in Christ.

Those who respond positively to the preached Word will not only have their lives altered in eternity, but also here on earth. The preached Word of Christ makes a more significant difference in what happens on planet earth than any other single factor. When Lord Robert Cecil was asked what he considered to be the most useful thing churches could do to aid the cause of world peace, he replied, "To preach the gospel." Shouldn't we believe that?

The arms race will not insure peace without transformed hearts. The gospel reconciles people to God and to one another. The preached gospel brings counseling and healing to people in the audience. The preached gospel actually affects the physical health of people. That is why it is called "sound" doctrine, for the word *sound* (as we have already discussed) refers to being healthy.

It is not enough just to proclaim words. To preach Christ is to apply His life-style to the situations we are going through right now. It is to allow God's Word always to be contemporary, to show how it relates to the computerized, highly technical, fast-lane, modern century. Preachers have a responsibility to bridge the gap between the meaning of the first-century Word and the situation of the twentieth-century world. And that type of bridge-building preaching keeps the gospel from being "dullsville." It guides, enlightens, protects, and leads us. Because of what the Word claims in 2 Timothy 3:16, 17, it must be preached "in season and out of season" (2 Timothy 4:2). We don't just do it when we *feel* like it or only when we do it in the professional way (from the pulpit or in the classroom). We are to communicate Christ in all kinds of situations we encounter during each day. We see situations as opportunities, and we beam Christ's way into those opportunities. There are various methods through which we can proclaim Christ—through correction, through rebuking, and through encouragement. But all is to be done with patience and careful instruction.

While the word *preach* often refers to communication with the non-Christian, the word *instruction* often refers to communication with Christians. Preaching enlists people into Christ; instructing builds up and matures them in Christ. While preaching primarily has to do with bringing a person to a saving relationship, instructing has to do with applying that salvation to daily situations of different habits, attitudes, actions, and reactions.

The charge was not just to "preach the Word." It also included the urgency of priority in every opportune situation, because men do not always want to hear sound doctrine. Instead of wanting to hear God's Word, some want to hear their own words repeated back to them (2 Timothy 4:3, 4).

There are four charges to Christian communicators in the midst of people with selfish ears. They include the *head, hardship, work,* and *duties* (2 Timothy 4:5). The head refers to what we think, and it is out of what we think that we will speak and act. Consequently, *our* heads must belong to *the* Head, Jesus Christ. We must not give our heads over to the changing situations. Instead, we must keep our heads full of Christ's truth.

Christians will face hardship, but instead of running away, we are to hang in there. The idea that Christians are to endure hardship stands opposed to what is being taught in many circles today—that Christians should drive better cars, wear better clothes and jewelry, and generally live the good life materially. That is self-centered teaching. It does not square with the Word of God. In fact, it belittles the community of unity that cuts across class distinctions and national barriers. Many Christians in other parts of the world haven't got the slightest idea what it means to drive a Cadillac, wear a Rolex, have a large bank account, or eat gourmet food—but they are committed Christians who follow the Lord.

Being a Christian in the midst of a changing world requires that we keep our heads, that we endure hardships, and that we *work.* It is work to introduce others to Christ. Isn't it interesting that those who belittle preachers because they are not involved in enough work do not resign their occupations and enter into the "easy street" profession? Ministry or service is not something we do because we get delightful feelings from it. We do it out of *duty.*

Duty comes out of obedience. While the work of an evangelist introduces people to Christ, the duties of servers are to meet needs. It is not an option. It is not something we vote on. We do what God requires out of a sense of duty and obedience.

The Model (4:6-8)

The apostle Paul is a model for preachers then and for today. He was one who gave himself as an unselfish offering for others in his ministry. He was not so hooked on the life-style of the present that he could not say good-bye to it. The word translated "departure" pictures a ship getting ready to set sail to other parts of the world. And Paul was ready to pull up the anchor, set the sail, and take his leave.

Paul was referring to his death. Elsewhere, he compared death to the moving from one house to another. While the sailing is leaving one place, it is going toward a new destination. Moving out of one house is to move into another. So Paul's departure was a movement to victory. He had fought the good fight. He had finished the race. He had kept the faith. And there was a reward waiting for him.

Notice that he "fought"; he did not desert. He fought the "good fight"—fighting the principalities and powers. The "bad fight" is fighting one another. Notice he "finished the race." He did not tire out and quit. He did not do improper things and get disqualified. Notice he "kept the faith." He did not change it, weaken it, water it down, ignore it, or let it go. Paul got involved (fought), he endured (finished), and he guarded (kept).

Victory awaits the winner. A crown was ready for Paul. In Christ, we are victorious. Christians are winners, not losers. Christians are crowned. Christians are rewarded, affirmed, honored, and promoted, either at death or when Christ returns—whichever comes first.

The Personal Request (4:9-18)

While Paul was in the presence of God (2 Timothy 4:1), he was still lonely for people. God created us to not only need God, but also to need other people. Paul affirmed that. He wanted Timothy to come to him as quickly as possible. Several had left Paul. Some had left him because they deserted the faith. Others probably left him because they had gone other places to serve.

Only Luke was with him. Luke was a physician and a dear friend (Colossians 4:14) who joined Paul's travels in the book of Acts. Luke probably joined Paul in order to be a physician for Paul's illnesses. If so, Luke was the first medical missionary. This was the Luke who wrote about the expansion of Christianity in the first century through his two-volume work, Luke and Acts.

The mention of Mark is a beautiful example of the reconciling nature of Paul. Paul's relationship with Mark covers five phases:

1. Mark traveled with Paul on the first missionary journey (Acts 13:1-5).
2. Mark deserted the work (Acts 13:13; 15:38).
3. Later, Paul denied Mark the opportunity of taking another journey with him (Acts 15:36-38).
4. Then Mark and Paul traveled on two different teams (Acts 15:39, 40).
5. Then Paul desired the presence of Mark (2 Timothy 4:11).

Why did Paul deny Mark earlier? It was probably to give Mark a sense of accountability. Mark had left the work at one time; and Paul knew that if Mark continued with that kind of life-style, he would never grow into maturity. Every time the going got tough, he might walk out. In order to teach Mark that accountability was expected and that he must learn to stick with his commitments, Paul denied him the privilege of working with him on the next trip. That denial no doubt ministered to Mark. He became more determined to stick it out, and he did.

Mark became precious to Paul; in fact, he became a benefit to him. Paul said, "He is helpful to me in my ministry." Aren't there times we have to say no to people in order to give them the direction they need to become the mature persons they can become?

Tychicus was a person who worked behind the scenes with Paul and for Paul (Acts 20:4; Ephesians 6:21; Colossians 4:7). The effectiveness of every modern-day Paul is dependent partly on the one who is willing to be a Tychicus.

Not only did Paul desire companionship, but he also wanted some comforts. He asked for his cloak (2 Timothy 4:13). This was probably a heavy outer garment that was also used as bedding. It is possible that Paul had no mat upon which to sleep and thus needed his cloak for warmth and also for bedding. Paul also wanted his reading materials. It is quite obvious that while Paul was expecting to be executed, he was not giving up. He intended to continue feeding his mind. To ask for the cloak was to ask for something for his body; to ask for the reading materials was to ask for something for his mind.

Paul did not camouflage people problems when doing so might have continued to hurt the body of Christ. He made it clear that a person named Alexander did him great harm and that Timothy should be on guard against him. The only reason that Paul would have brought that up was because Alexander evidently continued to spread his harmful activities elsewhere.

How many times have Christian leaders covered up a charlatan when that person should have been exposed for the protection of the rest of God's people? I heard of a church once that wanted to get rid of its preacher because he was damaging to the body, but they were in a dilemma. They did not know how to get rid of him, especially if they told the truth about him. So when another church decided to call him, the leaders of the first church disguised the problems by giving this kind of reference—"When you know him as we do, you will appreciate him the way we do." The second church heard one message—a positive one; but the church that was releasing him was really giving another message—a negative one.

Paul was not an exposer of just anyone that did not please him. In verse 16, he held out forgiveness to those who did not stick up for him during a trial period. We should be willing to let go of our grudges, hurts, littleness, bitterness, and disappointments. Jesus forgave on the cross. Paul forgave in prison. We need to forgive in our homes, shops, schools, and churches.

The first defense did not go well for Paul (2 Timothy 4:16), but it did not result in his execution. He was rescued "from the lion's mouth." This was a symbolic way of talking about the power of the judge, who could have ordered his execution at that time.

Even though Paul was expecting to receive orders for execution, it would really be an order to be rescued and brought safely to the "heavenly kingdom" (2 Timothy 4:18). Executioners do not have the last word about church leaders, God does. God preserves for eternity what the church's enemies persecute.

Final Words (4:19-22)

Paul finished this final letter of his life, not with complaints about the situation he was in, but with greetings to people who meant so much to him. Priscilla and Aquila were a fantastic couple who gave Paul a tent-making job when Paul came to Corinth alone. They traveled to Ephesus with Paul and set up a house church, then later had another house church in Rome. They evidently team-taught (Acts 18:24-28). Every time one was mentioned, so was the other. Here was a couple who did not run away from difficult situations, but purposely went to them for the purpose of bringing the grace and the peace of God to those situations. That was the case at Corinth, at Ephesus, and in Rome. Now they were back in Ephesus a second time—again in a difficult situation.

Onesiphorus was the person who sought Paul out in this second imprisonment and "was not ashamed of [Paul's] chains," which probably means he stood up for Paul (2 Timothy 1:16, 17). He may have verbally spoken against the Roman officials for imprisoning Paul, and it is quite likely that Onesiphorus lost his life because of it. That may be why Paul referred to his "household" instead of to him personally (2 Timothy 1:16; 4:19).

The universal nature of the gospel is seen by some of the people that Paul mentioned in these final greetings. Not only did he mention a married couple, the wife of whom was as significant in the spreading of the gospel as the husband, but also a city treasurer in Greece (Erastus), an Ephesian who accompanied Paul on his travels (Trophimus), a Roman senator (Pudens, according to tradition), someone who eventually became a bishop of Rome for twelve years (Linus—reported by Eusebius). We do not know who Claudia was, but some suggest she was the mother of Linus. Whoever she was, she must have been very significant in the ministry and life of the church.

Paul began his specific personal greetings by mentioning a woman and ended by mentioning another woman. Paul was not the male chauvinist that some think he was or that some of us ourselves have become. He was indeed a bridge builder.

Paul ended his writing to Timothy, who was living in the midst of a very difficult situation, with the equipping words, "The Lord be with your spirit. Grace be with you" (2 Timothy 4:22). All Christians have two spirits living within them. We have our own spirits and we have the Holy Spirit. The temptation is to ignore the Lord's Spirit and to live by our own spirits. Christian growth happens when we allow God's Spirit to so affect our spirits that it is no longer we who live, but Christ who lives in us. That means His characteristics, His attitudes, His responses, and His priorities dominate our total being.

The last words that we know were ever penned by Paul must dominate the character of the church in the midst of her struggles, interpersonal problems, heartaches, and temptations:

"The Lord be with your spirit. Grace be with you."

Part Three

Staying Put in a Tough Situation

Titus

INTRODUCTION TO TITUS

Crete: A Tough Place

Ever been in a tough place with regards to the church or your ministry? What do we tend to do? Don't we want to bail out?

Crete was a tough place for the church to be and, thus, a tough place for Christians to serve. One of their own spokesmen said about them, "Cretans are always liars, evil brutes, lazy gluttons" (Titus 1:12). When outsiders say something like that, we can wonder whether they really know the scene; but when insiders say that—get ready. It is probably even worse than they are revealing.

Crete was a mountainous island in the Mediterranean Sea. It was small—only 156 miles long and 7 to 35 miles wide. Being so small, there was no room for a person to get away. Since a negative environment can spread easily and rapidly, the whole island was a tough place for people to exist.

Crete was located south of Corinth and south/southwest of Ephesus. People from Crete were present on the Day of Pentecost (Acts 2:11); so there had been a history of Jews living on that island. Paul himself visited Crete on his way to the first Roman imprisonment; however, Paul's visit at that time was an unplanned visit (Acts 27:7-13, 21).

How did the church in Crete begin? It could have been started by those who were converted on the Day of Pentecost and returned to Crete. It could have begun by the seeds that Paul planted on that imprisonment journey. Or it could have begun from the efforts of other traveling Christians.

After Paul's imprisonment in Rome, he had evidently visited Crete again. But this time, he left Titus there to minister to the congregation (Titus 1:5). He wanted Titus to do a healing kind of ministry. When he said that he had left Titus there so that Titus "might straighten out" things, he was not saying he was to be a dictator. "Straighten out" was a medical term used to describe the setting of the bone that had been out of joint. It was a healing activity. In many ways, the church at Crete was sick and needed the healing touch of God's messenger.

There are several teachings that come out of this small letter:

1. Be willing to stay put in a tough situation. Everyday with Jesus is not always better than the day before. We have sweet days and sour days. We have cloudy days and clear days. Crete was a tough place, but Paul left Titus there because no tough place is impossible when a man of God stays put.

2. It is possible to have a church without elders. This church did not have elders, but it was still considered a church. It is better not to select men to be elders just to "have a church," if there are no men who are properly qualified. It is extremely dangerous to select elders too quickly. Instead of being quick to select elders, God's leaders must be committed to discipling people to reach eldership quality.

3. God's power, love, and grace are stronger than man's pollution, lying, and disgrace. It was out of the character of the Cretans—lying, evil beasts, lazy, and gluttons—that eventually elders would come with the characteristics described in Titus 1:6-9. Those men in the church at Crete did not grow up with those characteristics, but developed those good qualities out of the power of the presence of God's Spirit within them.

4. The church is not planted within a place to put a stamp of approval upon the life-style of that place. The church is planted by God in order to make a difference in the people's perspectives, practices, priorities, and destiny.

5. Paul developed three main things that are necessary to develop within the members of any church. Those three are godly leaders, godly teaching, and godly life-styles.

This little letter we have entitled "Staying Put in a Tough Situation." It might also be called "How to Be Effective in a Tough Situation." Being effective in a tough situation requires the following:

1. Be God's representative with unselfish motives—Titus 1:1-4.
2. Be a developer of people for leadership—Titus 1:5-9.
3. Be revolutionary or counter cultural—Titus 1:10-16.
4. Be relevant—Titus 2:1-15.
5. Be a reminder—Titus 3:1-8.
6. Be a reconciler—Titus 3:9-11.

CHAPTER FOURTEEN

Be God's Representative

Titus 1

Maintain Unselfish Motives (1:1-4)

Paul's description of himself has the necessary ingredients for a leader of God's people in any situation, including a tough location like Crete.

Servant

Paul referred to himself as both a servant and an apostle. Isn't it interesting that he did not link up apostleship with a controller or owner mentality? Paul rightly understood that the functional description of a true apostle is that of a servant. No one can be a good representative of Jesus Christ who does not wrap that up in the package of humble servanthood. Jesus himself was God's master servant. Jesus made it clear that anyone who wants to imitate Him should do it with the attitude of a servant (Matthew 20:20-28).

Our contemporary world tries its best to teach us the opposite. We are often told that the higher up we get in an organization, the less we ought to be serving the needs of people. We are told that elevation equals status, not service. Such an attitude will hurt a church, not heal it. It will destroy the harmony in the church, not protect it. It will model the devil's mind-set, not Christ's. It will cause leaders to become arrogant, not humble. It will cause leaders to become self-willed, not God-willed. Some characteristics of God-willed persons include unselfish motives, building up others, being divinely equipped, developing people, being a healer, and being able to spot leaders.

Unselfish Motives

Notice the purpose of the servant-leader Paul. What Paul did was "for the faith of God's elect and the knowledge of the truth that leads to godliness" (Titus 1:1). In other words, this leader's motives were not that people become addicted to him, but that they become addicted to God through faith, and to the truth through knowledge, and to Christ through godliness.

Faith and knowledge must be properly based, "resting on the hope of eternal life" (Titus 1:2). All of us have hopes tied to goals. We will trust in whatever we think will help us reach those goals. We will seek to know about whatever we think will help us reach our goals.

Eternal life means quality life—God's kind of life. It also means an ongoing life. Hope that rests on anything else is temporary. Too many leaders and too many Christians have been duped into resting their hope on getting rich, staying healthy, becoming popular, or some other earthly prize. All of that will fade away. A true servant-leader of God causes people to rest their hope on that which is eternal, and then helps people to reach eternity through faith, knowledge, and godliness.

Build Up Others

Paul built up Titus by calling him "my true son in our common faith" (Titus 1:4). He did not consider Titus to be a second-rate citizen or one with inadequate knowledge. Titus was a man of integrity, and his faith was the same as Paul's.

There are certain things that every Christian should have in common. No leader has a right to withhold knowledge or beliefs from others so that he has a special control over them. To talk about a "common faith" is to suggest that Christians in various denominational groups who wear different labels may still possess a commonness in their faith. That commonness is faith in Jesus Christ as the divine Son of God, who died, was buried, was resurrected, and lives for His people. That is "the faith that was once for all entrusted to the saints" (Jude 3).

Anyone with that "common faith" is a child of God and is a brother or sister to others. Whether or not we are true children (true sons) depends upon whether or not we maintain belief in that "common faith." There is a unity amid the diversity of God's people. That is why we pray "*our* Father."

There is an "ourness" with God himself. The first word of God in the Bible is *Elohim,* which is plural. It stresses the "ourness" of God's nature. God said, "Let *us* make man in *our* image." Indeed, all Christians are connected to one another because of this "common faith," and to affirm that connectedness is to affirm that we not only belong to God, but also to one another. Consequently, we should treat our brothers and sisters as true children of God, even when we may have differences of opinion on some issues. It is quite doubtful that Titus held the same opinions on all issues as Paul did, but he was still called a "true" child because of that "common faith."

Isn't it time Christians knocked down the walls that have divided us? Of course, we may meet in different places because we hold different opinions over some issues. But does that mean we have to cease seeing those who meet in other places as our true brothers and sisters in Christ?

Divinely Equipped

Paul did not leave Titus in this tough location with just human characteristics. He said, "Grace and peace from God the Father in Christ Jesus our Savior" (Titus 1:4). *Grace* refers to God's activities for our well-being, and *peace* refers to the result of God's activities in our lives—reconciliation with both God and man (Ephesians 2:17-22).

Effective ministry is not done by our own strength and methods, but by the presence and power of God. Our strength comes "from God the Father and Christ Jesus our Savior." Here is the source of our effectiveness. While we are looking for better methods, God is looking for better people. That is because God's methods are better people, and better people are those who are filled with God's grace and manifest God's peace. If grace is manifested in our lives, it will be expressed by forgiveness, acceptance of others, and consideration of others.

To be full of grace is to make our circle as large as Jesus' circle. A popular song of a few years back talks of one who "drew a circle that kept me out." That is the world's way, to exalt self by excluding others. But the way of Christ is different, as the song continues: "Christ and I . . . drew a bigger circle and took him in."

To be a person of peace is to be a person who does not fight the wrong battles. We are not to fight flesh and blood, but the principalities and powers in Heavenly places. Christians who meet in other places are not our enemies. Nor are our enemies non-Christians. They are prisoners of Satan, and our task is to free them from Satan's imprisonment. We do it with love toward them, not hatred against them. That is to manifest God's peace.

171

To be a person of peace means that we allow another to have a different opinion (Romans 14:1). To be a person of peace means that we become peacemakers by jumping over the sociological barriers that keep people apart from one another—those barriers caused by race, age, economy, occupation, and status.

Be a Developer of People (1:5-9)

It is not enough to just have the church grow; there must also be individual growth. The beach crowd on holidays grows; the theater crowd grows; the crowd at Disneyland grows; and with the same kind of marketing, the church crowd can grow. But *what* is growing? Maybe just the crowds, not the people.

We can have both types of growth, and God wants that. Out of garbage kind of people (Titus 1:12) can come God's recycling into steak-and-potato kind of people (Titus 1:5-9). That is God's dream. Let us not turn our backs on the social misfits. Let's let 1 Corinthians 6:9-11 happen again:

> Don't you know that the wicked will not inherit the kingdom of God? Do not be deceived: Neither the sexually immoral nor idolaters nor adulterers nor male prostitutes nor homosexual offenders nor thieves nor the greedy nor drunkards nor slanderers nor swindlers will inherit the kingdom of God. And that is what some of you were. But you were washed, you were sanctified, you were justified in the name of the Lord Jesus Christ and by the Spirit of our God.

Let's see Titus 1:12 turn into Titus 1:6-9 over again and again. It was out of the characteristics of verse 12 that we see the new characteristics described in verses 6-9. That was a living demonstration that the person in Christ is a new creation. The old has passed away. All things have become new (2 Corinthians 5:17). It happened in Crete, and it can happen in your community. It can happen in your family. In fact, it can happen to you.

In order for it to happen, the servant-leaders of the church will need to be committed to a life of discipling people into Christ-likeness. Persons were committed to doing that in Crete, or Paul would never have left Titus there to appoint elders. Without disciple-making, there would not have been anyone who was elder material.

An anonymous person has written the following about the ministry in the church:

172

Measure your success as Christian leaders not by the size of your congregation which may after all be only a huge ecclesiastical jellyfish drifting aimlessly and uselessly on the social sea, but by the stature and dimension of the manhood which you develop in individual believers, by the orderliness and serviceableness and Christlikeness of the separate disciples you build into Christian brotherhood.

Be a Healer

The words *straighten out* (Titus 1:5) were medical words in the first century that dealt with healing. Titus was to bring some healing to the situation there. Leaders must never be people who bring pain, hurting, alienations, or spiritual sickness to the church.

Be a Spotter of Leaders

We do not know how Titus went about appointing elders in every town. He may have selected them himself as a representative of an apostle. We have no clear-cut mandate in the Bible describing precisely how men are to be selected as elders. But one thing is sure—it would not be a popularity vote that would not take the characteristics seriously. The selection should probably come from spiritual people in the church. It could even come from spiritually-minded people from a neighboring church who also have these characteristics. It is interesting that here an "outsider" was given the responsibility to appoint elders. It certainly does not have to be that way, but it can be.

We have already discussed the terms *elder* and *overseer* in 1 Timothy; so I will not repeat that here. Some of the characteristics are also listed in 1 Timothy; consequently, I will discuss only those that were not mentioned there.

(a) A man whose children believe and are not open to the charge of being wild and disobedient (Titus 1:6). In 1 Timothy, Paul talked about children who obey the father and have proper respect for him. Here the children are to be believers in the Lord. The fact that they are not wild and disobedient shows that they have gone through a character change from their Cretan environment (Titus 1:12). Paul was talking about children who were at home, not about adult children.

Some people have disqualified men from being elders because their adult children are not living a life that expresses belief in the

173

Lord because of a negative, ungodly life-style. Surely we understand that in our complex society, children begin to listen to their peer groups, the mass media, their co-workers, and many others. When our children become adults, they have their own minds and can go astray. That does not mean that their father and mother were inappropriate spiritual leaders. If that disqualified men from being elders, would we want to disqualify God from being a good Father because some of His born-again children get off the track? Besides that, God's first two people did not turn out too well!

This qualification should not disqualify a man from becoming an elder after all of his children are grown and have left home. However, a man who is a Christian and has children at home should be the kind of spiritual leader that motivates his children to become believers in the Lord and have the resultant life-style. Unless he is that kind of father, putting him in an eldership role would be to take him away from his family so much that he might not be able to lead them into the same kind of faith-stance into which he is seeking to lead others.

Christian living and Christian service must begin at home, but it should not end there.

(b) Entrusted with God's work (Titus 1:7). Other translators say, "God's steward." A steward is not an owner, but a manager. God's servant-leaders must not think they are owners or controllers of the church. Some men need to leave some ownership at the altar and walk away from it and become humble managers of what God owns. Some men act as if they own the church and thus think they should control it. But the church is God's.

The chief characteristic of a steward is that he is faithful. He can be trusted. He is faithful to carry out the actions of the Master as well as the Master's attitudes. He is accountable.

(c) Not overbearing (Titus 1:7). Other translations say, "Not self-willed." He does not always have to have his way. He is not pushy for just his ideas, his programs, his gain. He is not a dictator. He is not obstinate or stubborn.

(d) Not quick-tempered (Titus 1:7). His fuse is long. That does not mean he never gets angry, but it means he does not get angry easily, nor does he stay angry for long. If he allows his anger to hurt others, he repents, confesses it, and asks for their forgiveness.

(e) One who loves what is good (Titus 1:8). The word *good* refers to what is beneficial. Elsewhere, Paul wrote that we are to

cling to what is good and hate what is evil. It would be inappropriate to choose a man to be an elder who loves what is not good—the wrong kind of music, the wrong kind of movies, the wrong kind of books, the wrong kind of magazines, or the wrong kind of entertainment. Isn't it interesting that this is a characteristic of an elder and yet is seldom evaluated when we choose men for this position? Few of us know what goes on in the private lives of the members of the church. Thus, it becomes important to spend enough time in dialogue and in contact with a man to find out what his priorities and practices are. It is too late to discover that after he becomes an elder.

(f) Upright (Titus 1:8). He is a man who has integrity. His conduct reveals that he loves what is good.

(g) Holy (Titus 1:8). This term refers to someone who is different. He does not cave in to the environment around him. His life is set apart to be Christlike. He does not go along with the crowd. He knows what it means to be different and is willing to remain different. Some people are different in that they are difficult to live with, but being holy means being different in morality—not strange in personality.

(h) Disciplined (Titus 1:8). He has his time, work, desires, and relationships under control. He is disciplined in his Christlikeness.

(i) Must hold firmly to the trustworthy message (Titus 1:9). He can encourage and build up others with "sound doctrine" (teaching that brings healing). He is not always chasing after a new fad, but he is always open, flexible, and teachable. The "trustworthy message" has to do with the divinity of Jesus Christ. Paul was not referring to the many opinions about Biblical teachings that float around. The elder is the one who zeroes in on Jesus. It is Jesus who saves and Jesus who unites. He does not get his eyes off-center; thus, he does not allow differences of opinion or differences over doctrinal issues to be divisive.

The reason these characteristics are required for God's servant-leaders in the church is that there are many "rebellious people" in the community who then get into the church (Titus 1:10). Consequently, God's servant-leaders must be counter cultural and revolutionary.

Be Revolutionary—Counter Cultural (1:10-16)

Christianity is not just to be relevant, not just to be contemporary, but it at times must be conflicting—that is, it must stand

against the negative and anti-godly cultural practices and principles. Often liberals are contemporary but not Biblical. Often fun-
damentalists are Biblical, but not contemporary. It is only when
the church is Biblical, contemporary, and conflicting that it is
Christlike. By conflicting, I mean real Christianity does not
become imprisoned by the life-style of the culture when that
life-style is counter Christ. Whatever there is in the culture
that is counter Christ conflicts with Christianity; Christianity
must then become counter cultural. Christianity must become
revolutionary.

Revolutionary Christianity will call for being wise enough to
know what is counter Christ (Titus 1:10, 12) and being willing to
risk being in conflict (Titus 1:11). Some people are mere talkers;
they are not much for "doing." They are deceivers, especially
those who push strict legalism. The church cannot be revolutionary unless it is able to spot that which is counter Christ; and it
must be willing to spot it and point it out, even though the majority are like that (as in Titus 1:12).

Paul commissioned Titus to silence such people because they
were ruining whole households by teaching what they ought not to
teach. In those days, groups met in homes, giving opportunity for
these deceivers to infiltrate these small Bible studies. They would
first be visitors and then become members for the purpose of
getting their side issues to become major teachings of those studies. Those people had to be silenced and rebuked, but with the
right motives—focus on faith, not faction (Titus 1:13); focus on
truth, not fads (Titus 1:14); focus on morality, not on popularity
(Titus 1:15); focus on good deeds, not on the sensational (Titus
1:16).

Notice the who, what, and why of the people that needed to be
changed. Such people today need to be changed as well.

Who They Were

They were the "rebellious" (Titus 1:10). They would not align
themselves with what was being taught; they had a counter idea.
They were not teachable. They were "mere talkers" (Titus 1:10).
They talked as if they had a special hot-line from God and could
write the Bible themselves. They were "deceivers" (Titus 1:10).
They were not what they appeared to be. They were legalists
("those of the circumcision group," Titus 1:10). They were the
"corrupted" (Titus 1:15). They did not see that anything was

pure. They were finding a sin underneath every rock. They were so negative that their minds and consciences were totally corrupt.

What They Did

They were "ruining" household Bible studies (Titus 1:11). They were like leaven and salt—just a little spreads fast. It was subtle and hardly noticed until the damage was done. These people majored in minors. They specialized in "Jewish myths." They were creative in understanding the Bible; they had all kinds of fanciful interpretations.

Why They Did It

They did it "for the sake of dishonest gain" (Titus 1:11). They did not do it for God, but for themselves. Some religious teachers get others so hooked on their fanciful interpretations, on legalism, emotionalism, and supposed messages from God that the people provide them with great wealth. It is easy to do that for someone else if you think that person is the only one who is right, is teaching you pure truth from God, and has a special hot line to God.

Some have captured the electronic media in order to multiply their audience and their gain. Some may do it for popularity, a following, status, recognition, and material gain. It is interesting to notice the types of homes, cars, clothing, jewelry, and activities some enjoy as the poor send in their contributions. Some are not nearly as interested in sharing the keys of the kingdom with others as they are in getting the keys to a new Mercedes or a new house or a new boat for themselves.

Paul summarized the description of this type of person by saying, "They claim to know God, but by their actions they deny him. They are detestable, disobedient and unfit for doing anything good" (Titus 1:16). *Detestable* referred to the relationship with others. Instead of loving others, they actually hated them. *Disobedient* referred to the relationship with God. *Unfit* referred to the relationship with self, spiritually out of shape. *For doing anything good* referred to the relationship with the environment; they were not benefiting their environment.

Conclusion

The church is in a tough environment indeed when its culture is characterized by people who are "always liars, evil brutes, and lazy gluttons" (Titus 1:12). It is even tougher when the church includes members who are rebellious, mere talkers, deceivers, wanting to fill their own pockets, rejecting the truth, and having detestable actions.

This calls for people who are committed to grow into Christ-likeness, become servant-leaders, and stay there. It is not time to run; it is time to stand. It is not time to quit; it is time to get to work. It is not time to be discouraged; it is time to encourage one another. It is not time to change ourselves to fit in with the culture; it is time to change the culture to fit into Christ's ways. It is time to be responsible and revolutionary as true representatives of God. After all, that is partly what it means for the church to be the body of Christ, the fullness of Him who fills all in all (Ephesians 1:23).

CHAPTER FIFTEEN

Be Relevant and Relational

Titus 2

On the one hand, while Paul cautioned about people who ruined households by teaching things they ought not to teach (Titus 1:11), on the other hand, he encouraged Titus to teach the things that ought to be taught (Titus 2).

Many people see the word *doctrine* as theology with its head in the clouds, but in this chapter we see that "sound doctrine" was always practical. The word *sound* means healthy or healing. The kind of doctrine that Paul outlined here was the kind that helps heal broken relationships.

Sound doctrine links teaching with life-style. It links beliefs with behavior. What we believe does make a difference, for out of our beliefs our behavior comes.

What disease is to the physical body, dis-easement is to the body of Christ. Paul discussed several attitudes and activities that bring healing to dis-easement.

The Fruit of the Spirit (2:1-10)

Several of the characteristics that Paul listed elsewhere as "fruit of the Spirit" (Galatians 5:22-24) are repeated in this section and are linked to the nitty-gritty, day-by-day interpersonal relational skills. They are self-control, faithfulness, love, kindness, and goodness. The only two not directly mentioned—peace and patience—are inferred in the words self-control and endurance.

The Older Generation (1-5)

For a long time, the church has put special emphasis upon its youth, and the church should do that. But at the same time, the church must not neglect the older members.

North America is graying. The average age of citizens in the United States is getting older and older. One study shows that by the year 2033, the life expectancy will be 120 years. Can you imagine the impact upon society and the church when people live at least one-half of their lives in retirement? There are now more people sixty-five years and older in the United States than there are teenagers. Some churches have added ministers for their senior saints.

The church needs the balance of both the older and the younger. The younger need to see the wisdom and practicality of the older, and the older need to see the innovative energy of the younger. Both need to see the other as important and needed in interdependency.

Sometimes, older people can get on tangents as they live a sort of second childhood. And to that issue, Paul told Titus to teach the older men to be "temperate." That means to have restraint in indulging desires. Temperate was originally used to refer to being moderate in the use of wine. Older people should not have so much time on their hands that they drink the time away. But this can apply to any activity of older people. Some older people can spend all of their time traveling in RV's, playing golf, taking trips to other parts of the world, or participating in various kinds of sporting or other recreational activities. In all of these activities, moderation should be the rule.

Getting older gives us no excuse for retiring from ministry. Older people should have the time to devote to ministry. Many of the ministries the young people are involved in can also be done by the older. For instance, older men could have various practical clinics in the church to help younger people, and particularly single mothers, in such areas as car repair, plumbing, electrical repair, carpentry, or other useful skills.

Older people are to be "worthy of respect." They should earn that respect by being self-controlled, sound in faith, loving, and enduring (Titus 2:2). Getting older is no excuse for getting grouchy. The longer a person lives with the Lord, the more reason he should have to be tolerant, helpful, gracious, loving, and stable. When older people give up on self-control, faith, love, and endurance, they may discourage the younger people from investing themselves in the life of the church. If life in Christ cannot withstand aging, then why should younger people want it?

The person who is self-controlled is the person who does not always have to have things his own way. The person who is sound in faith is one who trusts in God and does not spend a lot of time complaining that things are not as they used to be. A person who is sound in love is one who sees the needs of others and moves to meet those needs. Older people often have more time and more disposable income to meet those needs. A person who is sound in endurance is one who is not fickle. He does not run hot and cold. He does not hide when the issues get hot. He does not quit when he gets hurt.

As older men should not retire from Christian living, neither should older women (Titus 2:3-5). They should be engaged in activities dedicated to God ("reverent in the way they live"). The rest of what Paul said about the older women provided practical handles on which they could take ahold to express reverence. First, they were "not to be slanderers." Older women may have a lot of knowledge about people. Women are usually more verbose than men and more open to sharing feelings and situations. But a woman is not to be a talk-aholic. Nor are they to be "addicted to much wine." A woman is not to be an alcoholic.

These two negative commands are followed by one positive: they are to "teach what is good." Older women have much experience that can be passed on to younger women. The "good" that Paul referred to here has to do with a younger woman's beneficial relational skills in both the home and society. Thus, Paul went on to elaborate on some of what these older ladies were to teach the younger.

In Society. These women were instructed first to teach the younger women "to be self-controlled and pure." What practical teaching this could include. Some younger women think older women have never been tempted to be unfaithful or impure or faced the pressures that they face. Isn't it time that we become more transparent in the church? What a ministry it would be if older women would share with the younger how they have worked through stressful temptations and situations in their lives. It would also be helpful for the older to teach the younger how to maintain their self-control when all is falling apart. How to get through it without throwing pans when the kids are sick or the plumbing doesn't work.

The second lesson was "to be kind." It is not easy for a young woman to be kind when the weather, the kids, and even the appliances seem cruel. But kindness includes looking beyond the household for other people who have special needs. It is a woman's disposition to be sensitive to other people who have hurts, needs, setbacks, and tragedies. But the kindness to other people in such situations provides a live-in model for the watching children, teaching them to grow up with a kinder attitude about life.

In the Home. With so many attacks on the modern family as we face today, what advice could be more relevant than this? First, they were to teach the young women "to love their husbands and children." While some women may say that loving husbands and children is such a natural manifestation of wives and mothers that no one needs to teach it, the apostle would not agree. There are many practical handles for loving husbands—in his social, intellectual, recreational, and sexual needs. Many older women can teach younger women significant practical advice about loving children through the various stages of life that children go through—from infancy through adolescence. How did the older women handle those days? How did they relate to their children when they were rebellious? What kept them going when they seemed to be at their wits' end?

Second, they were to teach them "to be busy at home." This does not mean the woman has to stay at home all the time. But when she is at home, how can she organize her day so she can get the most done in the least amount of time? Some young women end up wasting a great deal of time because they don't know how to organize it. They never seem to have time to have a tidy house, clean laundry, as well as some quiet time to themselves. Time management is as important to the young, busy mother as it is for an executive. In some cases, it is even more important, for she has no secretaries or assistants.

Finally, the older were to teach the younger women "to be subject to their husbands." This does not mean to render blind obedience, but it does mean to give up self-centered interests for the well-being of the husbands. Lest many women are concerned about this being unfair, we need to remember that the apostle Paul said that submission is mutual; we should submit to one another (Ephesians 5:21).

The reason for older women to teach younger women is "so that no one will malign the word of God." Unless we get our behavior down, people will think that the teachings of God, the character of God, the mind-set of God is not helpful in the practical issues of life. Christians are living epistles, read by all kinds of people (2 Corinthians 3:2, 3).

Many churches have applied this teaching by offering classes on specific topics taught by older women or by having question-and-answer sessions with a panel of older women.

The Younger Generation (6-8)

The younger generation can be so impetuous. They are not often patient with the slowness of the church to adopt new methods, new music, and new ministries. Sometimes, the younger set acts without planning well. It is out of that background that Paul instructed Titus to encourage young people to be self-controlled (Titus 2:6).

Isn't it interesting that Paul told Titus to teach the older generation several things, but he did not talk about teaching the younger generation? Could it be that the younger generation is not as open to being taught as the older generation? Is it possible that the younger think they know everything? So over against verbally teaching the younger generation, Paul encouraged Titus to be an example in front of them. That meant that Titus would have to spend time with them in relational activities.

Some things were "taught" to the older generation while other things were "caught" by the younger generation. Notice what the older and younger are to do that are similar. Both are to be self-controlled, both are to be serious ("temperate," Titus 2:2), both are to have soundness of speech ("not slanderers," Titus 2:3), both are to show integrity ("sound in faith," Titus 2:2). So both the young and the old were to be good examples—"so that those who oppose you may be ashamed because they have nothing bad to say about us" (Titus 2:8), or "that no one will malign the word of God" (Titus 2:5).

The inference here is that the younger generation will better catch on to the Christian life-style if it is modeled by the older. The word translated "example" literally means to be a type or pattern. It originally meant an impression made by a dye. So older people are to make an impression upon the younger that molds their behavior patterns.

I saw a good illustration of this once in Thailand. Monks would make rubbings over engravings on walls and then sell them. (These "rubbings" were copies of the wall engravings, made in a manner similar to the way one can copy a penny by placing it under a paper and then rubbing over it with a lead pencil. The image of the penny that appears on the paper is a "rubbing.") In the same way, young people should be able to rub their lives up against the older people and have the impression of Christlikeness imprinted in them. We learn from one another in our relational activities. "As iron sharpens iron, so one man sharpens another" (Proverbs 27:17).

For the older people in the church, the advice is, "Be careful, the younger generation is watching and they may follow." For the younger people, it's, "Pay attention. Follow the good examples before you."

Christian Employees (9, 10)

Although we do not have slaves today, this section (like 1 Timothy 6:1, 2; see the comments on that passage, above) has significant application to the employer-employee relationship. Employees are to be subject to their employers in everything—and that is super tough. This, of course, does not mean that we are to be subject to them to the extent that we would engage in immoral practices. But it does mean that employees are to give up self-centered interests for the well-being of their employers. It refers to such things as to the quality of work that they give while at work, the way they talk about their employers behind their backs, the way they talk about the product of their employers, their willingness to go the "second mile" even though extra pay might not be coming, to be thoughtful in carrying out the policies of the company. Paul then lists some ways that express submission to the masters.

1. "Try to please them." Many times employees think the employers should please them with all the benefits possible, but it first of all begins the other way around.
2. "Not to talk back to them." This deals with the complaining, argumentative person. Some employers know what it means to have employees who are eternal gripers.
3. "Not to steal from them." Employees can steal in many different ways—the unauthorized use of the telephone, taking too much time for lunch and coffee breaks, taking home office supplies like pencils, paper clips, or paper, stealing the employer's reputation by talking about the company's situation, and calling in sick when one is not sick. The employee can steal time, quality of work, reputation, materials, and fringe benefits. Anytime an employee embitters another against the employer, he is also stealing loyalty.

4. "Be fully trusted." That means being trusted with materials, time, work products, other employees, and outsiders.

The reason the Christian employee is to relate to the employer with respect is the same as the reason for Paul's advice to the older and younger generations. It is not that the employee will stay out of trouble; it is that "in every way they will make the teaching about God our Savior attractive" (Titus 2:10). The attractiveness of the teaching about God is not restricted to a church building on Sunday morning, but is also to be present at the place of work Monday through Saturday.

Actions that draw the following reactions of non-Christians— "That no one will malign the word of God" (Titus 2:5), or that they will "be ashamed because they have nothing bad to say about us" (Titus 2:8), or that they see the "teaching about God . . . [is] attractive" (Titus 2:10)—are mostly applied and expressed after we leave the church building, in the home, in the streets, in the marketplace, in the factories, and in the offices. If it does not happen in those places, then it probably does not exist, regardless of the game that we play with our pious talk.

Christianity must not be reduced to "trivial pursuit." That is, being overly concerned about the order of worship, the volume of the music, the time of the services, who serves the Lord's Supper, the type of hymn book used, the dress of the choir, or any of a hundred other things we can fuss about. The Pharisees were the inventors of such pursuits, but effective Christianity never deals so extensively with the trivial. Effective Christianity is demonstrated by the day-by-day life in all kinds of relationship situations. Effective Christianity is the fruit of the Spirit in action.

The Rootage for the Fruitage (2:11-15)

The fruitage of the Christian life (Titus 2:1-10) comes out of the rootage of Christian teaching (Titus 2:11-15). A person can live the life-style that Paul has described because "the grace of God . . . has appeared to all men" (Titus 2:11). That grace of God equips men with the presence of God, the power of God, and the provisions of God.

The reason people can be self-controlled and live in purity as Paul outlined is because the grace of God teaches us to say no to ungodliness and impatience. The reason Christians can live in endurance and in submission to others is that we know this life is temporary—we live in the hope of the "glorious appearing of our great God and Savior, Jesus Christ" (Titus 2:13). The reason Christians can live unselfishly with the good of others in mind, as Paul has outlined, is that Christ himself is the example "who gave himself for us." If Christ gave himself for us, then we can give ourselves up for others in various day-by-day relationships because that same Jesus lives within us.

Paul made it clear that Christ gave himself for us, not just so that we could go to Heaven but also to redeem us from a negative life-style here and now (Titus 2:14). The main doctrines of the church, including grace, salvation, redemption, and the second coming of Christ are all calculated to make a difference in the way we live today and tomorrow. (See *grace* and *salvation* in verse 11, *redemption* in verse 14, and *the glorious appearing* in verse 13, and then relate these truths to the way we live in the present age).

God's grace refers to His activities for our good. It refers to anything He does for us to equip us to live for Him right now with His life-style. God's grace *saves* us—"brings salvation" (Titus 2:11). That salvation is wholistic. God saves us from sin, death, exposure, loneliness, self, depression, destruction, unloveliness, laziness, the devil, demons, enemies, environment, and everything else that would enslave or destroy us.

God's grace *guides* us—"teaches us to say 'No' to ungodliness and to worldly passions" (Titus 2:12). Temptation comes to all of us; we are tempted by our own desires (James 1:14). But God never allows us to be tempted beyond what we are able to endure; He will always provide a way of escape from any temptation that the devil hurls at us (1 Corinthians 10:13).

Not caving in to temptation involves the commitment to say no. It involves a fleeing (1 Corinthians 6:18). It involves resisting and standing firm (1 Peter 5:9). It involves watching and praying (Matthew 26:41). It involves drawing near to God (James 4:8). It involves confession (1 John 1:9). It involves being filled by the Spirit (Ephesians 5:18). It involves being led by the Spirit (1 Thessalonians 5:19). It involves testing (1 Thessalonians 5:21). It involves avoidance (1 Thessalonians 5:22). It involves imitating the life of Jesus, who was tempted in every point as are we (Hebrews 4:15). God has indeed taught us how to say no to temptations. But the question comes, "Do we want to say no?" We might say maybe, but to say maybe is as practically unwise as to decide to stay in an airplane that is in a nose dive. We must be very determined and committed to say no.

God's grace *empowers* us to live in our environment with God's character—"self-controlled, upright and godly lives" (Titus 2:12). That is the power of God's Spirit, who lives within us. We can live upright lives because God has placed His *sperma* in us.

God's grace gives us *hope* (Titus 2:13). Many people are living hopeless lives. Without hope, why manifest discipline? Without hope for tomorrow, who cares how we live today? No hope, no heart.

Hope is never passive. Real hope is always active. It is based upon evidence; if it is not, then what is called hope is really superstition or subjective feelings. Suppose I come home to my wife and say, "Julia, my mother is going to be visiting for three weeks." If she asks how I know that and I answer, "Oh, I just have a feeling," then Julia would not do much to prepare for the visit. But if I said to her that my mother called and is now at the airport, then the hope becomes active. Julia would start getting her room ready.

We have undeniable evidence that Jesus Christ died, arose, and will be coming back. The person who has that hope begins to purify himself now for that life in Heaven (1 John 3:2, 3). That is active hope. We pray about it, "Thy will be done *on earth* as it is in heaven."

God's grace *sacrifices* for us—"who gave himself for us" (Titus 2:14). God has always been a sacrificing servant and Lord. He calls us to be living sacrifices here and now (Romans 12:1).

God's grace *redeems* us (Titus 2:14). To be redeemed is to be purchased. Christ purchased us for God by His own sacrifice on the cross. The Christian is God's property. Thus, God will protect the Christian, care for the Christian, provide for the Christian, and take the Christian home to Heaven to live forever. We are His, and we are to live like it.

God's grace *purifies* us—"to purify for himself a people" (Titus 2:14). To be pure does not mean we are perfect, but it does mean we are forgiven. But that is not all there is to it. God also changes us to live differently. When we purify water, we make it fit for others to drink. When God purifies us, He makes us fit for others to see Christ in us. He not only forgives us, but also cleanses us and is doing a new work in us.

God's grace also *motivates* us—"eager to do what is good" (Titus 2:14). Much of the world is eager to do what is bad. Christians must bring God's balance by having more eagerness to do what is good. May Christians not allow the pagan world to out-motivate us.

Many times our Christian teachings major in issues that do not make that much difference in how people live their lives. Is it possible that too much of our teaching zeroes in on our hobby-horses? And is it possible that we do that just to convince other people that we are right and they are wrong, and thus should change their church membership to ours? Is it possible that much of our teaching does not make application to the nitty-gritty living that people go through everyday?

The first-century message must walk around in twentieth-century clothes and ride on the freeways, look into microwave ovens, work on the assembly lines, figure insurance, and fix computers.

A recent Gallup poll indicated that never has there been so much Christian teaching in this country while at the same time having so little impact upon the life-style of the people. Does that mean we are really majoring in minors and minoring in majors? Are the things that upset us the things that make very little difference in godliness, purity, and Christlikeness? Would that be the reason for the Gallup poll results? We dare not weaken the impact of the application of the Christian teaching to whatever social situations in which we find ourselves.

That was the reason Paul said to Titus, who was in an extremely difficult environment, "These, then, are the things you should teach. Encourage and rebuke with all authority. Do not let anyone despise you" (Titus 2:15). That was not just for Titus then. It is also for Christians today.

CHAPTER SIXTEEN

Be a Reminder and a Reconciler

Titus 3

Isn't it easy to forget? God knows that and has given us many reminders. For instance, the Sabbath day is a reminder that this world belongs to God because He created it in six days. The rainbow is a reminder that God will never again destroy all of life by a flood. The Lord's Supper is a reminder of Christ's death, resurrection, and His promise to return, and that His family is united in Christ. Preaching and teaching are to be reminders of truth we already know as well as communicating new truth.

Be a Reminder (3:1-8)

A Reminder of What Christians Are to Be (1, 2)

Christians are to be good citizens, "subject to rulers and authorities" (Titus 3:1). Christians have no right to be subversive, but they do have the right to use legal means to voice their concerns and disappointments. Paul frequently took advantage of the privileges of his Roman citizenship. He forced a public apology in Philippi (Acts 16:37-39) to vindicate the gospel. He refused to be flogged in Jerusalem (Acts 22:23-29) so that he could present his case fairly. And he appealed to Caesar rather than cave in to a mindless mob action (Acts 25:9-12). Christians today are similarly free to take advantage of their citizenship for good.

Christians are to be models of obedience to traffic laws and paying taxes. Citizenship also involves being "ready to do whatever is good." That means being cooperative in matters that can benefit the communities in which we live. Christians should be volunteering for many civic projects, running for the school board, and being presidents of their local PTAs. If it is good, Christians ought to be at the head of the list and be models of doing it, while not seeing it as competitive to service in the church.

The attitude of Christians should be seen in the use of the tongue—"to slander no one" (Titus 3:2). Christians are called by God to be ministers of reconciliation (2 Corinthians 5), but it is extremely difficult to be a model of reconciliation if all the while we are using the tongue to build up walls between people.

The positive tongue comes from a positive disposition—"to be peaceable and considerate" (Titus 3:2). *Peaceable* refers to someone who is not always ready for a fight. He is filled with compassion, not contention. He carries the sword of the Spirit, not the spirit of the sword. He brings harmony, not harassment. The Greek word translated "considerate" is a word that refers to a person who has himself under control. He does not allow things to upset him easily. It is a word that describes a previously wild horse that is now tamed. That horse is usable, not just living for itself.

A mark of Christian citizenship also includes "true humility toward all men" (Titus 3:2). Notice two key concepts. One concept is "true." It is not a false humility, but one that is genuine. It comes from the inside out. The other key concept is "all men." The Christian has no prejudices. He does not automatically put certain people into categories and ignore or mistreat them. The Christian follows the Father's example of being "no respecter of persons."

A Reminder of What Christians Were (3)

The Christian life-style as a citizen comes from being a changed person. There is a noticeable difference between what a Christian is to be and what he was. We can see that connection easily, as demonstrated on the following chart.

Present (Titus 3:1, 2)	Past (Titus 3:3)
Subject to authorities	Foolish, disobedient
Obedient	Disobedient
Ready to do good	Deceived, enslaved by passions and pleasures
Slander no one	Malice
Peaceable	Envy
Considerate	Hated and hateful
Humility toward all men	Hating one another

Paul was reminding Christians that conversion does not only change position, but also practice. It does not just change beliefs, but also behavior. It does not just change doctrine, but also deeds. Conversion is not to be lived out only in church services, but also in communities. Real conversion makes a difference in the way a person thinks, lives, and relates to others.

A Reminder of What Christ Did (4-7)

The movement from the past to the present is due to the kindness and love of God. He saved us. That is, He saved us from all of the negative attitudes and activities in verse 3. He saved us in all these ways:

1. By what He is in His character—"kindness," "love," and "mercy"—which lives in us (Titus 3:4, 5).
2. Through "rebirth" (Titus 3:5). That birth is from above. New birth comes with forgiveness. With forgiveness, one's whole life starts all over again. It is as if he had never sinned. In that new birth we are connected to Christ and one another. In that new birth old things have passed away—all things have become new.
3. Through the "renewal by the Holy Spirit" (Titus 3:5), which means two things. (a) The Holy Spirit has been renewed in us. God has given us His own Spirit. (b) That Spirit renews our inner man. While the outer man is decaying, the inner man is being renewed day by day (2 Corinthians 4:16). In that renewal, we have returned to man's original form—the image of God, God's full nature living within us as a seed.
4. By the death of "Jesus Christ our Savior" (Titus 3:6). Because Jesus was perfect, He took our place on the cross. Our sins were laid on Him. And by His stripes, we are healed, inwardly healed.
5. By justification (Titus 3:7). That means just as if we had never sinned.
6. "By His grace" (Titus 3:7). Salvation is not something we earn or deserve. God granted it out of His desire and love. His grace is so magnificent that when God forgives us of our sins, He forgets about them entirely. He will not embarrass His children by spilling the beans when He comes back. The slate is wiped clean. That is grace.

He has written our names as "heirs" in His will. Consequently, we don't have to be jockeying for position because all that is the

Father's will be ours; we can devote ourselves to doing what is good here and now. We don't have to grab; we can give. We don't have to envy; we can be generous.

Be a Reconciler (3:9-11)

Crete was filled with problem people, and problem people need a positive example of a peacemaker who will not cause divisions and who will not tolerate people who do. Titus was to reflect reconciling attitudes that included staying away from arguments about legalism and refusing to give in to a devisive person.

"Avoid foolish controversies . . ." (Titus 3:9). These arguments are "unprofitable"; they do not bring people to Christ and are useless in maturing people in Christ. Those who live for a good fight find themselves involved in controversies rather than conversions, in arguments rather than *agape,* and in quarreling rather than building up others.

"Warn a divisive person . . ." (Titus 3:10). Titus was not to give in to divisive people. Christ died to unite His people; the devil specializes in bringing disunity into the church and will use negative people to do that. Church leaders have been wrong to cater to those divisive people. In order not to offend them, we often allow them to continue with no rebuke. As a result, they upset and offend others. A divisive spirit is like gangrene. It spreads; it is never satisfied. It poisons and destroys by pitting one person against another. It is so serious that such a person should be disfellowshipped for continuing to do it: "Have nothing to do with him" (Titus 3:10).

We don't hesitate to do that with our physical bodies. Though it is painful, we will use surgery to cut away a part of our bodies that is harming the rest. We do not let toxic malignancy take over. Neither should we allow it to grow in the body of Christ. Christ is the head of His body, the church, and He deserves to have a healthy body.

Some people refuse to confront a person who has a divisive spirit because it is not the "kind" thing to do. But it is not kind to allow Christ's body to be infected and stay sick. Christ went through enough pain on the cross. Let's don't give Him more by allowing divisive people to dominate.

A person who majors in bringing disharmony into the church is a pawn in the hands of the devil, for the devil specializes in divisiveness. That is why Paul said such a person is "warped and sinful; he is self-condemned" (Titus 3:11). The number of times a person comes down the aisle or the length of time he has been a member of the church does not automatically measure his spirituality. However, a person's attitude toward unity and disunity denotes whether or not he is Jesus' disciple. A Christian will not wish to do anything that would hinder the effectiveness of Jesus' prayer for unity in John 17.

The Christian leader has some attitudes and activities to avoid (Titus 3:9) and some people to warn (Titus 3:10).

Conclusion (3:12-15)

After Titus's initial ministry in Crete, Paul intended to send a replacement, either Artemas or Tychicus. Paul knew the need for "R and R" (rest and relaxation) for someone who was on the front lines in a hot situation. As Paul had poured himself into Titus in a discipling role, he would continue to do that. He asked Titus to join him at Nicopolis. There Paul would no doubt build Titus up, encourage him, equip him, and inspire him.

Evidently, this letter had been hand carried to Titus by two people—Zenas and Apollos. Paul reminded Titus to be sure to see that these two special ministers had everything they needed while in Crete and were given financial support for their next assignment (Titus 3:13). It was a custom that Christians provide finances sufficient enough for the next journey of traveling ministers, messengers, and evangelists.

Paul concluded his letter by re-emphasizing one of his major teachings to Titus; that is, the people must commit themselves to doing what is good in the midst of a very antisocial and sinful environment. When people all around are liars, evil brutes, lazy gluttons (Titus 1:12), the counter cultural life-style of "doing what is good" must shine out of a determined devotion, commitment, dedication, and discipline (Titus 3:14).

Do you ever feel as if you are all alone? And nobody cares that you are hanging in there for Christ? Paul wanted to be sure Titus knew that *people* appreciated him and cared: "Everyone with me sends you greetings." And he wanted him to know that *God* cared: "Grace be with you all" (Titus 3:15).

Here is the flip side of the two great commandments. When Jesus was asked which was the greatest commandment, He responded with two. The first is to love God; the second is to love our fellowman (Matthew 22:37, 39). That is not the only direction love goes—to God and others. We also must know that love comes *to us* from others—"everyone with me sends you greetings." Love comes to us from God—"grace be with you all." What a support base for tough situations!

Paul began this letter by reminding Titus what kind of leaders the church in Crete needed and closed it by outlining what kind of support that servant-leader needed. That support comes from God and from others.

We can know that we are recipients of love from those two sources. Let us receive that with thanksgiving, humility, and acceptance. But may we also know that we are to be vessels of God's love to those who are in tough situations today. We are to send them our greetings; God's grace touches them partly through our reaching out to them.

When people are in tough situations, it is as if they are on an island all by themselves, separated from many of their brothers and sisters. That is especially true on the foreign mission field. Let us close the gap—whether of distance or culture or situation or whatever. Let us dig holes, plant poles, and string wire to communicate our greetings and God's grace—communicating with those individuals and with God on their behalf.

Part Four

A Bridge Builder

Philemon

INTRODUCTION
TO PHILEMON

Paul's Situation

Paul was in prison when he wrote this letter. This imprisonment was certainly not the same one as when he wrote 2 Timothy. When he wrote that letter, he expected to be executed. However, Paul was expecting to be released from this imprisonment (Philemon 22). In addition, Demas was called a "fellow worker" (Philemon 24), but Demas had "deserted" Paul by the time 2 Timothy was written (2 Timothy 4:10). This was probably the imprisonment that we read about in Acts 28:30, 31, when Paul was in a house-arrest imprisonment, which gave him great freedom to receive people. People could come and go and perform special ministries for Paul.

The Situation of Philemon and Onesimus

Philemon was a dear friend of Paul and a fellow worker in a church (Philemon 1). He was a benevolent person as seen in Paul's reference to his love for the saints (Philemon 5). He was involved in evangelism and, thus, would have been very receptive to hearing that someone else had become a Christian. Philemon was evidently a convert of Paul and thus indebted to him for sharing the gospel with him (Philemon 19). Philemon was evidently wealthy and had slaves.

Onesimus was one of Philemon's slaves, but had run away. He may have stolen from Philemon in order to have resources to run away and get far enough. He got as far as Rome and somehow met Paul, who evangelized him. Onesimus then began to serve Paul, but at some time decided to confess his runaway slave situation. In good conscience, Paul could not keep Onesimus. No doubt in mutual agreement with Onesimus, he sent Onesimus back to Philemon with this intercessory letter.

The Nature of the Letter

Both a Personal and a Church Letter

While at first it looks as if this is strictly a private letter between Paul and Philemon, it is more than that. While it is personal, it also goes beyond the personal. Not only was this addressed to Philemon, but it was also addressed to two other people—Apphia and Archippus—as well as to the entire church that was meeting there (Philemon 1, 2).

A Revolutionary/Counter Cultural Letter

What Paul requested in this letter was revolutionary in the first century. For a slave to run away was a serious matter. When a runaway slave was found, he was treated in several different ways. Many were beaten or tortured. Some were branded with a hot iron to indicate that they had been fugitives or runaway slaves. Some were executed. But against all of that, Paul was asking Philemon to forgive Onesimus and to receive him as a useful brother, not as a mistreated slave.

Some are concerned that Paul did not say more against slavery in this letter. What Paul did say about slavery was as revolutionary as would have been accepted in the first century. Paul spoke about slave/master relationships in Ephesians 6:5-9 and Colossians 3:22-25, and what he said was revolutionary.

There are several reasons why Paul did not express himself as harshly on the subject of slavery as some would like. Much of the slave/master relationship was far different from what many Americans envision. In many circles, the slave/master relationship was more like the employee/employer relationship today. Some of the most educated people at that time were slaves, and some of the most significant functions—such as medicine, school teaching, and law—were done by slaves. Many slaves were well treated, well paid, well respected, and sensed a well-being about their situations. But even with all of that, being a runaway slave was a serious matter. It was somewhat like being A.W.O.L. in the military today.

The abolishment of slavery must come from the inside out; if it does not, rebellion will result. To condemn slavery significantly might have caused many slaves to revolt, which would have resulted in murder and violence. Paul was more concerned about the proper care and relationships among people than the social status people had within those relationships. Paul's letter was calling for Philemon's Christian principles to be the determining factor over cultural expectations.

An Intercessory Letter

Here is a model example of one Christian interceding for another Christian with no benefits coming back to the intercessor. Christians need to engage more in this kind of activity. We must not think that another Christian's problems are his only. Christians are brothers and sisters in the same family. Consequently, we have responsibility not only to God, but also for one another.

God's question to Cain is still God's question to us, "Where is your brother?" Cain's response should not be ours, "Am I my brother's keeper?" Instead of asking that question, Christians should make a determined statement, "I am my brother's keeper." After all, Jesus interceded for people when He was on earth (Luke 22:32). And Jesus is still interceding for His people (Hebrews 7:25; 9:24; Romans 8:34). And the Holy Spirit is interceding for us (Romans 8:26). Should we do anything less? To be a disciple of Jesus is to be willing to stand between people who are at possible risk and be a bridge builder. Bridge building may be the most important function of people on earth.

Possibly the Laodicean Letter

When Paul wrote the church at Colossae, he referred to a letter that he had written to Laodicea. He asked that those two letters be shared between the congregations (Colossians 4:16). The Archippus mentioned in Colossians 4:17 is probably the same as in Philemon 2. It is possible that Archippus was in Laodicea, and the brethren in Colossae were to deliver Paul's message (Colossians 4:17) to Archippus as they delivered the letter to Laodicea and received the other letter from Laodicea. If so, this letter could be that letter, which Archippus would deliver to the Colossians.

Some significant scholars feel that Paul's advice to Colossae to encourage Archippus to "see to it that you complete the work you have received in the Lord" referred to reconciling Philemon and Onesimus. It is certainly true that Archippus was involved in the decision-making process, as well as the whole church that evidently was meeting in Archippus's house (Philemon 2).

The slave Onesimus seems to be identified with the Colossae brethren (Colossians 4:9). But some have suggested that the cities of Colossae, Hierapolis, and Laodicea were so close together that Christians in those cities made up one single church, although meeting in various houses. If all of that fits together (and there are admittedly some problems with it), this letter to Philemon could be the lost Laodicean letter.

A Reconciling Letter

The primary thrust of this letter was for reconciliation between two people. It called for forgiveness when wrong had been done. It called for the acceptance of another person as a Christian brother, even though he was from a different class distinction.

A Persuasive Letter

There are many elements of persuasive speech in this letter. None of these was added to be manipulative, but out of concern for someone else. Used properly, these are legitimate persuasive characteristics:

1. A commendation to a person. Paul addressed Philemon as a "dear friend and fellow worker" (Philemon 1).
2. Including others in the situation. No one does anything as a "Lone Ranger" (Philemon 2).
3. An appeal to a person's benevolent characteristics (Philemon 5).
4. An appeal to the writer's personal situation—in prison and aged (Philemon 1, 9).
5. An appeal to personal relationships (Philemon 17, 19).
6. An appeal to practicality (Philemon 11, 16).
7. An appeal to forgiveness (Philemon 16).
8. An appeal to what this meant to Paul personally (Philemon 12, 16, 20).
9. An appeal to the best side of Philemon (Philemon 1-7, 14, 21).
10. An appeal to a follow-up visit (Philemon 22).
11. An appeal to personal indebtedness (Philemon 19).

The Outcome of the Letter

Later tradition tells us that this same Onesimus became a bishop of the Ephesian church. We do know as a matter of fact that a person named Onesimus did become a bishop at Ephesus. Whether this is the same person or not, we do not know for sure. But there is no reason to believe that it could not have been.

CHAPTER SEVENTEEN

A Bridge Builder

Philemon 1-25

Paul's Greeting (Philemon 1-3)

Paul called himself "a prisoner of Christ Jesus," and there is a sense in which all of us should see ourselves as "prisoners" of Jesus. We are to be captured by His love, by His mercy, by His characteristics, and His ministry. When we are captured by Him, He liberates us for meaningful living.

Everyone is a prisoner of someone or something. A person can be a prisoner to his feelings, to his peers, to success, to education, to the desire to be accepted, to sins, to habits, or to desires.

There are two words for *prisoner* in the Greek language. One refers to being in bonds. That is the word used here in verse 1. The other word refers to being a prisoner of war; that word is used in verse 23. Both of these words suggest that Paul was in bonds (in chains) because of a warfare. Indeed, Paul considered himself to be in warfare. He was in a spiritual battle, just as we must be.

Timothy was with Paul. Although Paul includes Timothy in the greeting, the rest of the letter is from Paul personally, as seen in the times he used the word "I" instead of "we." Paul picked up the word *our* in the relational dimension—"Timothy, *our* brother," Philemon *our* dear friend and fellow worker," "Apphia *our* sister," and "Archippus *our* fellow soldier."

There is to be a sense of community among Christians. There is an "ourness" within the Christian family that is to take a priority over a "me-ness." We are to make decisions for the good of the whole, not just for the good of the individual. Paul began his letter to Philemon, emphasizing the community aspect of the family of God, as seen in the little word *our*. That could have made a significant impression on Philemon as he considered his responsibility toward the runaway slave who was now a Christian and a part of "our" group.

Paul did not write this letter to just one individual, but to the church, for this decision would have an impact on the whole church. Onesimus had become a Christian, and as a Christian, he had a right to the fellowship. The church had to take the responsibility for fellowshipping with him; so Philemon's relationship to Onesimus would have an impact upon the community.

We do not know exactly who Apphia and Archippus were. Some suggest that Apphia was Philemon's wife and Archippus was their son. If so, the letter was to the family, of whom Onesimus was a slave. If Onesimus were a household slave, Philemon's decision would no doubt include the others in the family.

This letter also included the whole church that met in their house. It is quite possible that Onesimus did significant services for the church when it met in the house. Now the church would need to see Onesimus not just as a slave, but also as a brother.

Having house churches helped enhance church growth in the first century. Church buildings did not appear until the third century. Today, many churches are taking advantage of the Biblical concept of people's meeting in homes for prayer, singing, Bible study, and even the Lord's Supper. Cottage prayer meetings and cell groups meeting in homes are becoming quite prevalent. A church in Korea has a membership of over a half million because of the evangelistic efforts of house groups all over the city of Seoul. Some people are reluctant to have these small groups because they feel they can't keep control over them when they are meeting in different homes during the week. It is time to relinquish the control and allow God's Spirit to release the church to grow so that people are added *daily*—not just once a week.

Philemon would not make this decision only on the basis of the persuasiveness of Paul or on the counsel from his family and the church; he would also be equipped by God for this decision. That equipment is wrapped up in the words *grace* and *peace*.

Grace refers to God's activities for our good; *peace* refers to the absence of alienation that we have with God, ourselves and others. It is difficult to claim the grace of God unless we extend that grace to others. It is difficult to claim peace with God if we do not allow reconciliation in broken relationships to happen. So grace and peace were significant for Philemon's ongoing relationship with Onesimus. It would not mirror Christlikeness to see Onesimus as a brother around the Lord's table but treat him as less than a brother the rest of the week.

A Thankful and Praying Paul (Philemon 4-7)

Isn't it interesting that though he was prison, Paul was thankful? Notice what he was thankful about. He was thankful about God's people—their faith and love. There is a relationship between having "faith" in the Lord and having "love for all the saints." God does not call us to have a relationship only with himself or only with others. The two go together like wings on the fuselage of an airplane and like gasoline in an automobile. It is contradictory to the Christian system to meet together, expressing our faith in God through prayers, praise songs, and preaching while nursing animosity toward the people sitting next to us.

Do you have faith in the Lord? Then it should be seen by your love for others. Love to others involves risk, sacrifice, expenditures—all of which require trust, trust in God, trust that our risk will not destroy us, trust that our sacrifice will not weaken us, and trust that our expenditures will not bankrupt us. We trust that God's grace is sufficient for the love we render to others.

Paul did not end his prayers with only thankfulness, but also with requests. Notice what he asked for. He was a prisoner, but he did not ask to be freed, to have finances, or to have the comforts of home. He asked that those who were not in prison be "active in sharing your faith" (Philemon 6). And if they did it with the purpose that they would "have a full understanding of every good thing we have in Christ," they would be more willing to be reconciled with others. What we have is the result of Christ's gifts to us; what we have is the result of Christ's compassion to us, His grace to us, and His forgiveness to us. As we freely receive, we should freely give those characteristics to others.

Philemon had a reputation for ministering to the hearts of the saints (Philemon 7); so it was easy for Paul to approach Philemon with a request for reconciliation with Onesimus. There are some Christians who are not easy to approach for the benefit of another. Wouldn't it be wonderful if all of us could grow in grace, in peace, in faith, and in love so that others would know that we are approachable to become benevolent to people who have wronged us—even when they did it knowingly and intentionally?

Paul's Bridge Building (Philemon 8-22)

Paul could have demanded that Philemon receive Onesimus back, but God wants cheerful givers—not those who give out of compulsion or guilt. Using sheer authority to push through what is right can build walls and weaken relationships. Making requests with an appeal through *agape* can break down walls and strengthen relationships.

Paul did not use his authority as an apostle to make demands. Isn't that a model example for elders, deacons, and other leaders of the church today? Shouldn't we make requests and allow God's grace and Spirit to work on people? That will call for trust in God and people; it will also call for patience. It will mean that we do not insist on having our own way, but work to enable others to grow up in Christ's way. What would happen to the harmony of the church if more people would quit trying to be controllers and instead become models of compassionate service?

What would happen to the "community of unity" in the church if we would "appeal" to certain ones for the sake of others (Philemon 10)? Onesimus had been converted by Paul while Paul was in prison and began to serve him in helpful ways (Philemon 10, 11). The word *Onesimus* literally meant useful or profitable. After becoming a Christian, he began to live up to his name.

Paul could have turned Onesimus in to the government; then the legal authorities would have sent him back to Philemon. Instead, Paul, with the cooperation of Onesimus, sent him back not as a slave to a citizen in the Roman political legal sense, but as a Christian brother to a Christian brother (Philemon 12). Christianity must live above the political barriers that can keep us from each other. Christianity must live above the cultural expectations, some of which build gaps instead of bridges.

What a heart Paul had—to be willing to give up what was valuable and useful to him for the sake of another brother. What a heart Paul had to say, "I do not want to do anything without your consent, so that any favor you do will be spontaneous and not forced" (Philemon 14). Perhaps every member of the church should memorize that verse and let that be a motivating verse for our relationships toward one another. To be able to live like that with others will call for an increase in love—love that is patient, kind, doesn't act ugly, doesn't seek its own, is not easily provoked, does not keep score of wrongs done to it, and manifests all the other qualities of 1 Corinthians 13.

When Paul said, "I am sending him," he used a word that also meant to refer a case to. Paul may have been saying, "I am referring this case back to you." He would not decide about this by himself; he would not demand that his way be followed.

Sometimes it is difficult to see the good amidst the negative. But we should see every situation through the eyes of Romans 8:28, "And we know that in all things God works for the good of those who love Him, who have been called according to His purpose." Paul saw the situation through those eyes when he said, "Perhaps the reason he was separated from you for a little while was that you might have him back for good—no longer as a slave, but better than a slave, as a dear brother" (Philemon 15, 16).

Our reactions will largely be conditioned by how we look at things. Some people can look at the same thing and have different reactions because they "see" differently. We need to help one another see the potential positive amidst the present negative. That was what Paul was doing with Philemon.

Paul did not camouflage his feeling about the situation. Too many times we have hidden agendas when we approach someone, and they may never know what it is. Paul would not play those games. He made it clear that Onesimus was dear to him, and that to welcome Onesimus would be the same thing as welcoming him (Philemon 17). If we only knew how many times hurting one person hurts others as well. We might slow down on insisting on having our own way.

Paul not only went to bat for Onesimus, but also was willing to take personal responsibility for him, "If he has done you any wrong or owes you anything, charge it to me" (Philemon 18). This was not taking away Onesimus's own responsibility, but it was taking seriously and personally the fact that Onesimus probably had no physical means for any reimbursement. Whatever Paul would be charged because of Onesimus's debt would be small in comparison to the debt Philemon owed to Paul. Philemon was indebted for his eternity. That is more precious than gold and silver; that cannot be stolen, devalued, or traded away.

Paul wrote in confidence that Philemon would indeed continue his Christian benevolence and, in doing so, would refresh Paul's spirit in prison. People are more prone to live up to the trust we have in them if we express that trust. The opposite of trust is coercion. Coercion leads to animosity.

Paul asked Philemon to reach out in forgiveness to a person who did wrong. We must be willing to accept others who have been unacceptable to us. We must be willing to forgive others who have hurt us intentionally and with premeditation. We must be willing to receive people who have been rascals. Vengeance belongs to the Lord. He will repay. Forgiveness also belongs to the Lord. He wants to issue forgiveness through us. He wants us to leave vengeance to Him and express forgiveness for Him.

In Paul's request for Onesimus, he was not asking Onesimus to run from his past, but to face it and to rise out of it. He was asking Philemon not to be embittered by what had happened, but to be bettered by it. He asked him to receive Onesimus back as someone useful, as a brother, and as better.

Isn't this a classic example of how we should not lock people into their past? We should not categorize people according to how we knew them to be at one time. We should not entrap people into their previous immaturity and insensitivities. We should be open to what the grace and peace of God can do.

Few letters show the heartbeat of fellowship as does this one. Regardless of what Philemon did, Paul expected to visit him (Philemon 22). Paul did not say, "Unless you fulfill this request, I will never visit you again." His fellowship with Philemon was based upon Christ. Paul's relationship with Philemon continued through mutual prayers. Paul had prayed for Philemon (Philemon 4), and Paul was sure that Philemon was praying for him (Philemon 22). No wonder there was a sense of partnership and friendship and mutual trust.

Closing (Philemon 23-25)

The situation between Philemon and Onesimus was known beyond Onesimus's immediate acquaintances. Paul's fellow prisoners knew about it and sent greetings to Philemon. Christians are connected to other Christians. Even the Lone Ranger needed Tonto. And we must express that connectedness through our concern and responsible fellowship with each other.

It is a shame that we live in the midst of the most connected world in history (we are connected to other parts of the globe electronically), and yet we are a most disconnected people. Many church members are disconnected from one another. Let us be bridge builders. Let us be open so that the grace of God may be with our spirits, that His grace may be seen in the community of people reconciled to God and reconciled to one another in spite of their differences, in spite of their past, in spite of their sins.

That is what the church is all about. And that is what Paul's letter to Philemon was all about.

It is a little letter with a big heart. May it enlarge ours!